Creating Drama with 7–11

This practical book gives you all the ideas you need to make drama a regular and integral part of your school's curriculum, offering detailed suggestions of drama work for ages 7–11. The teaching units are arranged around four strands: drama for literacy; drama and the whole curriculum; drama, film, media and ICT; and drama for performance. The authors provide a wealth of practical activities throughout. Each unit includes:

- explicit links to the *Renewed Framework for literacy* and the wider curriculum;
- a list of resources needed;
- clear learning objectives and outcomes;
- steps for teaching and learning, including how to modify activities to suit your school;
- links to writing;
- assessment guidance.

Based on the authors' experience as teachers and in-service trainers, this book provides a wide range of ideas and activities for inspiring drama across Key Stage 2, and is essential reading for all those interested in bringing drama into their school.

Miles Tandy and **Jo Howell** are advisers with Warwickshire's Educational Development Service, UK. They have written widely about drama and literacy, and their publications include *Creating Writers in the Primary Classroom* (Routledge, 2008) and *Beginning Drama* (Routledge, 2008).

Creating Drama with 7–11 Year Olds

Lesson ideas to integrate drama into the primary curriculum

Miles Tandy and Jo Howell

Routledge
Taylor & Francis Group

LONDON AND NEW YORK

First published 2010
by Routledge
2 Park Square, Milton Park, Abingdon, Oxon OX14 4RN

Simultaneously published in the USA and Canada
by Routledge
711 Third Ave, New York, NY 10017

Routledge is an imprint of the Taylor & Francis Group, an informa business

© 2010 Miles Tandy and Jo Howell

Typeset in Goudy and Trade Gothic by Wearset Ltd, Boldon

British Library Cataloguing in Publication Data
A catalogue record for this book is available from the British Library

Library of Congress Cataloging-in-Publication Data
Tandy, Miles.
Creating drama with 7–11 year olds: lesson ideas to integrate drama into the primary curriculum/Miles Tandy and Jo Howell.
p. cm.
1. Drama in education. 2. Drama–Study and teaching (Primary) 3. Interdisciplinary approach in education. 4. Education, Primary–Curricula.
I. Howell, Jo, 1972- II. Title.
PN3171.T365 2010
372.66–dc22   2009022754

ISBN10: 0-415-56259-7 (hbk)
ISBN10: 0-415-48350-6 (pbk)
ISBN10: 0-203-86434-4 (ebk)

ISBN13: 978-0-415-56259-1 (hbk)
ISBN13: 978-0-415-48350-6 (pbk)
ISBN13: 978-0-415-86434-0 (ebk)

To Mr and Mrs Reeves: dedicated teachers of drama

Contents

Contents

Acknowledgements

Our sincere thanks are due to all those teachers and their classes who
have helped develop these materials: those who have lent us their
classes; those who have tried some units out; those who have read
drafts and made suggestions and comments. Also to all our friends
and colleagues at the Educational Development Service for their
support, professionalism and friendship. Thanks also to members of
the education department of the Royal Shakespeare Company,
particularly Mary Johnson, Rachel Gartside and Jacqui O'Hanlon, all
of whom have had a profound and lasting effect on our work. Finally,
thanks and love to Denise and Gideon for their support and patience
throughout.

How to use this book

Recent years have seen a growing interest in the place of drama in the primary school. Many of the teachers with whom we work recognise drama as a very powerful way of engaging children in learning right across the curriculum. Drama offers a very natural and accessible medium through which children can experience, explore and present ideas. They use their bodies, their voices, and the spaces and objects around them to investigate, understand and make. With skilful and sensitive teaching, children can cheerfully tackle ideas and concepts in drama that they might find much more difficult through talk and writing alone. And perhaps most important of all, drama can offer children some of the most engaging, rewarding and joyful experiences that they can have together in their primary schools.

Although many of the teachers with whom we work would share these sentiments entirely, many also tell us that sustaining drama teaching over a whole school year is challenging to say the least. Teaching drama often requires levels of skill and confidence that go well beyond those which most teachers have been given in their initial training. Even if you have been lucky enough to receive some in-service training in teaching drama, you may have found it difficult to sustain your initial enthusiasm once you have used all the strategies and ideas you were given on your course.

So the purpose of this book is twofold: to provide you with plenty of ideas for teaching drama across the age range; and to offer you step-by-step guidance for putting them into practice. *Creating Drama with 7–11 year olds* gives you and the other teachers in your school a comprehensive programme of drama teaching and learning. You may wish to use it exactly as it is set out in these pages, but it has also been designed to allow it to be used flexibly, moving and adapting units to fit with your curriculum, even designing completely new units if you need to.

If you are new to teaching drama with this age range, you may find it helpful to use these units in conjunction with one of the other practical guides we suggest in Appendix 2. Ideally, you may also want to get some good-quality in-service training for you and the rest of your staff. Like many teachers, once you start making drama a regular part of your teaching practice, you won't want to stop. These units have been carefully designed to make sure that you never have to.

The four strands

Year group	Drama and literacy	Drama and the whole curriculum	Drama, film, media and ICT	Drama for performance
Year 3	*Gentle Giant*	The Romans	*Dr Xargle's Book of Earthlets*	All about our town
Year 4	*Theseus and The Minotaur*	Change in the environment	Space	*A Comedy of Errors*
Year 5	*The Listeners*	Howard Carter and Tutankhamen	*The Invention of Hugo Cabret*	*Sir Gawain and the Green Knight*
Year 6	*Leon and the Place Between*	Shipwrecked: making for survival	Silent film	*Coriolanus*

Figure 1

Figure 1 shows the four units for each year group. These are stranded under the headings of: drama and literacy; drama and the whole curriculum; drama, film, media and ICT; and drama for performance. The strands in this book build on from *Creating Drama with 4–7 year olds* to give a cohesive and comprehensive programme right through the primary phase. The strands are inter-related and have been designed so that the understanding from one unit will reinforce the others for that year group.

Strand 1: Drama and literacy

Teaching children to read and write remains, quite rightly, one of the most important purposes of primary education. Drama has a very particular capacity to bring the teaching of literacy to life; giving children imagined experiences which enrich their reading and writing. The renewed *Primary Framework for teaching literacy and mathematics*, which is currently used in most English primary schools, explicitly encourages the inclusion of drama to immerse children in literature and give them experiences that will support their writing. The Framework also includes objectives for speaking and listening, including drama. These objectives are included in the drama and literacy strand, but also appear in all the other strands too.

Strand 2: Drama and the whole curriculum

All drama has to be about something, and drawing that content from the curriculum you will be covering anyway can be a very effective way of making best use of the limited time you have available. Drama can also make a unique contribution to bringing curriculum content alive and making it relevant and meaningful for young children. Once you have taught these units, you will find that the structures and strategies you develop can be applied to all sorts of other curriculum content as drama becomes a natural part of teaching and learning in your classroom.

Strand 3: Drama, film, media and ICT

Film, television and computers are all important sources of learning and entertainment for children. Rather than underestimate the potential of these media, or dismiss them as 'sitting in front of a screen', this strand shows how drama can work with them to help children be active, creative agents with such media, making content rather than just consuming it. Because good drama involves children being up on their feet and moving most of the time, it can greatly enrich their engagement with film, media and ICT.

Strand 4: Drama for performance

Children's performances for others in school, for their parents, and for other members of the community, can be some of the most exciting and rewarding times in the cultural life of the primary school. This strand shows how performances can be integrated into your programme for drama, building on children's ideas and ambitions to create high-quality work of which everyone can feel proud.

How the units are organised

The units follow a common structure from Year 3 through to Year 6. They are designed so that you can find your way through them quickly and easily, following the ideas exactly as set down where you want to, perhaps picking from them and adapting them as you become more confident. They are organised under the following headings:

Where this unit fits in

In this section you will see how the unit links to the rest of the curriculum and to the other units for the year group. This is designed to help you at the planning stage, so that your work in drama is integrated fully with the rest of your curriculum. If the work is based on a book, film, play or other story, you will also find a concise synopsis of the plot.

Key learning

The first section under this heading sets out the Key learning for drama. These are the objectives specific to drama which will help not only to keep the work focused as you go through the unit, but will also guide the criteria against which you will assess children's work. As the unit progresses, you will also be carrying out informal assessments of where groups and individuals are, so these objectives may need to be adapted and refined as you go.

You will also find learning objectives from the *Primary Framework for teaching literacy*. There will always be at least one of the drama objectives included, but the work in the units also covers some of the objectives for speaking, listening, reading and writing. These are included only where they are likely to form a significant focus in your work.

Resources

This section includes requirements for the space or spaces you will need to work in, including whether they will need to be blacked out, etc. You will also find lists of any other props and items of costume required so that you can put these together before you start. Pens and large sheets of paper are often needed, but are not always specifically listed in the resources section – it is a good idea to have these around at all times.

Steps for teaching and learning

This is the section where you will find detailed instructions for putting the unit into practice. The structures and activities are outlined step-by-step, rather than specifying them lesson-by-lesson. How long you spend in an individual lesson will vary from school to school, perhaps from one class to another. Even your own lessons may vary in length according to how much time you can make available, the stage the work is at and the particular needs of the children. Some teachers will want to undertake the work quite intensively, perhaps over a few days or a week or two. Others may want to fit the unit into a term or half-term of weekly drama lessons – there is no fixed way in which the units must be taught. You will need to integrate them with whatever planning systems your school has in place, but it is always good to keep in mind that the quality of the children's work matters much more than the paperwork. Photocopying and annotating the unit may be all you need to do.

Although the steps for teaching and learning are clearly set out, the exact course the work takes will depend very much on decisions that you and the children take as the unit progresses. This is particularly true of the performance units where what is offered is more a structure for devising work with children, rather than an exact recipe for the eventual product. There are no ready-made scripts because the intention is that you and they will devise them together as you go. Although the unit on *The Comedy of Errors*, for example, might be done each year, the approach taken and the form of the final performance may vary considerably from one year to the next.

You will find that the units refer to a number of dramatic structures and conventions. The more drama you do in school, the more these will become part of the language that both teachers and children use to plan and talk about their work. A full list of these strategies, with a brief explanation of each, is included in Appendix 1.

Guidance on assessment

With all the detailed assessment you need to carry out in other areas of the primary curriculum, it can be very difficult to make assessing drama a priority. However, if you want to value drama and give it the status it deserves, you need to be able to give as clear an account as possible of what children have learned and how they are progressing. The objectives set out under the 'Key learning for drama' heading will guide your observation, assessment and recording of children's work. In this section, you will find the objectives listed again, along with some prompt questions for each to focus your assessment. You are very unlikely to want to record detailed answers to these questions for all the children, but you may want to record something about those that performed very well during the work, and/or those who found it difficult to engage. But we have deliberately not included complex assessment and recording processes or burdensome paperwork. Your school will already have its own assessment policy and practice in place: the intention of the guidance in this section is to help you gather the information that you will need to fulfil your school's requirements.

Linking to writing

All teachers will be familiar with the complaint, 'I don't know what to write about!' Because good drama immerses children in deep and rich imagined experiences, it can provide a fabulous stimulus for writing. Children will often use richer and more complex language in drama and role play than they might in their everyday talk, so it can have a very significant impact not just on what they write about, but also on the language they use. It is important to stress, though, that this rich language needs to be 'caught' and recorded *at the time*. All too often, children will be full of rich language and exciting ideas as they leave their drama lesson, only for those ideas and language to have evaporated when they settle down to do some writing. This is why we make the links with writing explicit, and suggest that you keep large pens and sheets of paper to hand all the time. A few moments spent recording ideas not only gives you a valuable resource to use back in the classroom, it can also provide a quick and energising change in activity during your lessons.

Adapting this unit

As we have already suggested, the units in this book can be taught exactly as they are set out to provide a comprehensive programme for drama. However, you may find that they do not fit exactly with your other curriculum plans and that you need to make some adjustments to meet your school's needs.

Moving a unit from one year to another should present you with relatively few problems. You will need to look at the objectives and adjust them for a different age group, but the other units should help you do that. There may also be some changes in the steps for teaching and learning to make the activities appropriate for the new age group.

In this section we also give some guidance should you want to adapt the unit for different content: another book may be integral to your plans for literacy, for example, or your other curriculum plans may specify different coverage. The more confident you become with teaching drama, the easier these adjustments and adaptations will become. As you and the rest of the staff become more experienced and confident, you will probably find that you can use the skills and experience you have developed from working your way through these units to devise and teach units of your own.

Above all, the intention is that the units we offer here should allow your drama curriculum to get off to an exciting and practical start. Once drama has become a natural and everyday part of the way you all work, you will find that the units grow into a curriculum that is truly your own and that genuinely meets the needs of the children that you teach.

3L | *Gentle Giant*

This unit is based on *Gentle Giant*, by Michael Morpurgo, illustrated by Michael Foreman, Collins, ISBN 0-007-11192-4.

Where this unit fits in

Gentle Giant is the story of a young man who lives all alone on an island in the middle of a lake near the village of Ballyloch. His mother died when he was very young and, without any human contact, he has never learned to speak. A giant of a man, the villagers fear and ridicule him, calling him 'The Beastman of Ballyloch'.

One day he rescues a young woman, Miranda, from drowning in the lake. They fall in love, but the girl's father forbids her to see him.

Then a 'smiling stranger with twinkling eyes' arrives in the village and convinces the villagers to sprinkle his magic stardust on their lake so that they can catch more fish. They do catch fish, but the lake soon turns slime-green and stagnant. The Beastman notices that when he lifts Miranda's straw hat from the water it brings some of the slime with it. This gives him the idea to use straw to clean the lake. It works, the lake is clean and fresh again and the Beastman is reconciled with the villagers and reunited with Miranda.

This unit might also connect to:

- other work you are doing on contrasting localities – this is the story of a small, isolated community who depend on their immediate locality to survive;
- other work on the environment and sustainable development;
- work in RE on the significance and symbolism of water;
- PSHE work related to the ways in which we treat others, feelings of isolation and resolving conflicts.

Key learning

Key learning for drama

By the end of this unit, the children will have:

- explored the ways in which they can communicate meaning through body language and facial expression;
- told and explored parts of the story using still images;
- explored the central character's dilemma through a simple version of forum theatre;
- represented and explored the behaviour of the crowd as they respond to the 'smiling stranger'.

Primary Framework for literacy objectives

- Drama – use some drama strategies to explore stories or issues.
- Engaging with and responding to texts – empathise with characters and debate moral dilemmas portrayed in texts.
- Creating and shaping texts – use beginning, middle and end to write narratives in which events are sequenced logically and conflicts resolved.

Resources

NB: all the resources are optional and the drama will work without them if necessary. They are:

- an overhead projector to project an image of the Beastman and images of the village;
- a table with poles fixed to each corner and a selection of cloths and other objects to represent the Smiling Stranger's cart;
- a recording of water to use as background sound;
- a selection of scrap paper, self-adhesive notes and labels, and large, coloured pens.

Although some of the teaching ideas in this unit can be used effectively in the classroom, you will also find it helpful to have access to the hall. You may also want to make use of the outdoors to help you explore the sounds, textures and atmosphere of the island.

Steps for teaching and learning

Step 1: Speaking without words

This story provides the teacher with an opportunity to explore the power of physical, non-verbal communication. The Beastman has never learned to speak, but he seems to have the ability to read human mannerisms, even from a distance.

Children should each have a partner. They should be distant from each other so that, when prompted, they can look at each other across the room. On the command 'Go', children walk around, looking for spaces, weaving in and out of each other, but always trying to stay distant from their partner. The teacher then calls out a word or phrase that describes an emotion, e.g. *anger, distress, fear, loneliness, confusion,* at which point the partners will stop and hold each other's gaze in the manner of the word. The teacher then says, 'Go' and they walk on again, until the next word is called.

Ask the pairs to each give themselves a letter 'A' or 'B'. On 'Go', they walk around the space again, but this time, rather than calling out an expression, the teacher will simply call out 'And stop'. 'A' has to communicate an emotion of their choice to 'B', without speaking. They hold the gaze until the teacher says 'Go'. Children continue to walk until the teacher says 'Stop' at which point 'B' acts out a silent response to the expression that they have just seen from 'A'. The activity continues in this way, each pair building one emotion on top of another. This enables the class to explore the different subtleties of language and expression.

Each pair is then given a pad of adhesive labels. They are given two minutes to write down as many ways as they can to describe the expressions and emotions they built up in the game. There should be one word or phrase per label. For example:

angry   *confused*
threatening   *defensive*
ready to attack *ready to fight*

or

tight shoulders   *raised eyebrows*
raised fists   *standing straight and tall*
lurching forward *fingers tightened into hard fists*

After the two minutes, the children can look at the words or phrases they have jotted down. Now they can move them around and order them, so the weakest expressions are on the bottom, the strongest on the top.

Step 2: Life and the lake

The silver lake is central to the lives of the villagers and is the source of much that they need. Yet it is also what separates and isolates the Beastman from the rest of the community. In your discussions around

4

this unit, you may also want to explore the importance of water in all people's lives, and its deep significance and symbolism in many religions.

Children work in groups of about four or five. Begin by making a series of images which explore the importance of the lake to the villagers, showing how they use it for a range of everyday needs: collecting fresh water, fishing, travelling and transporting goods. Words and movement can then be added to the images to make living 'captions'. Emphasise the need for the language used in these to be poetic rather than everyday, for example 'Our lake is fair and full of finest fish' evokes a sense of place much better than 'We get fish from the lake'. The first caption is also an example of the iambic pentameter. If you simply set the children the challenge of having exactly ten syllables in their caption, you and they will be surprised and delighted by the language that emerges.

Step 3: The Beastman

Starting from some of the language in the text – *The Beastman's coming! – Look out, look out, Mister Ugly's about! – He's mad. He's bad. – He'll gobble you up for his supper. Don't go near him* – create still images to show how the villagers react to the Beastman. The teacher can then take on the role of the Beastman, walking through the images, with each coming to life with some words as the Beastman passes by. To protect individuals, it is important that the teacher takes this role rather than one of the children.

Pick out the phrases that the villagers use to describe the Beastman. He cannot speak, yet somehow he understands that it is dangerous for him to leave the island and meet the other people across the water. Explore how different textures in voices can be used to convey meaning.

Project a picture of the Beastman on the wall, using an overhead projector.

The children should stand at the other side of the room from the projection. They are going to taunt the image, but they are only allowed to say the word 'Beastman'. Each time they say 'Beastman' they must create an action which moves them closer to the image. This works best if the teacher challenges the children to taunt him in different ways. For example, 'Taunt him using only soft voices ... show anger in your voices ... show fear and confusion in your voices.'

As the children move closer and closer to the image with their words and actions, a silhouette should begin to emerge in front of the projected image. When they are close enough, the pupils should be encouraged to stop and hold the very last action, so that a dramatic shape has been created. If the teacher feels the children are ready, they could even be encouraged to create a beast shape from the shadow of their own actions.

On self-adhesive notes or scrap paper, children make quick jotted observations about the sounds that would reach the Beastman from across the water. Mark out an area that represents the sea and ask the children to stick their notes on 'the water' – e.g. *scratchy*, *harsh*, *high*, *squeaky*, *breathy*, *snarling*, *sneering*, etc.

Step 4: The rescue

After you have read the relevant part of the story, the children work in pairs to devise ways of miming the rescue of Miranda by the Beastman. They can enact these as you read the story again, then you can experiment with adding music to what they have made, perhaps using more than one piece and discussing the effectiveness of each.

Step 5: Miranda and her father

After her rescue and meeting with the Beastman, Miranda's father is furious and locks her in her room. Using very simple props (tables, chairs, etc.), the children can create Miranda's room, then use scraps of paper to add information (e.g. *a draughty window looking out over the lake, an old straw doll,* etc.) and place these around the 'set' they have created.

One of the children can then take the role of Miranda, and the teacher the role of her father. The rest of the class form lines to make a square that represents the walls of Miranda's room. Using a simple version of forum theatre, the children's job is to help Miranda persuade her father to let her go to visit the Beastman again. Miranda and her father enact their argument/discussion, but the action is paused periodically for the children to comment and suggest ways ahead. At these points, you may also change the child who is playing Miranda, but the central purpose will stay the same.

Step 6: The Smiling Stranger

Read the relevant passage from the book, then create a simple version of the Smiling Stranger's cart using a table, a few cloths and some poles or sticks fixed to the legs of the table to make the covering. With the rest of the class forming the crowd, children (perhaps in pairs or threes) can take turns with the role of the Stranger and experiment with the language he can use to persuade the villagers to buy his magic stardust.

In pairs or threes, children are given coloured paper cut into the shapes of bunting flags. On each flag they write words and phrases which made them really feel they wanted to buy the stranger's magic dust. These are then clipped to strings or ribbons coming from the corners of the cart, creating 'buntings' of persuasive language. For example:

all you ever wanted   the richest in the world
the best you could buy   magic powers

The buntings can then be taken and displayed in the classroom to support children in their writing.

Step 7: Thanking the Beastman

Use similar structures to Step 3, where the villagers expressed their dislike and fear of the Beastman. Project a picture of the Beastman's island on the wall. In groups of three or four, the children create images of the villagers moving towards the island, pausing and calling out their thanks.

The last step is to play some music (something that you already use for country dancing would do very well) and create the villagers' final celebratory dance. If you pause the music, the children 'freeze' the dance and call out words and phrases to represent how the villagers are feeling at the end of the story.

Guidance on assessment

Any assessment of this work will be related back to the Key learning for drama, which stated that by the end of this unit the children will have:

- explored the ways in which they can communicate meaning through body language and facial expression – *how successfully did they do this? Who played the games really well and who seemed to find them challenging?*
- told and explored parts of the story using still images – *were the images clear? How much variation was there between them?*
- explored the central character's dilemma through a simple version of forum theatre – *who joined in and offered ideas? Did they commit to any roles they were asked to play? Who offered interesting insights during and after the forum theatre activity?*
- represented and explored the behaviour of the crowd as they respond to the 'Smiling Stranger' – *how effective was this? How varied were the children's contributions and reactions?*

Linking to writing

There are plenty of writing opportunities that arise from this work including:

- diaries – Miranda, the Beastman, villagers;
- poetry – starting from some of the language used in the captions in Step 2;
- dialogue – between Miranda and her father after you have done Step 5;
- adverts – for magic stardust!

Adapting this unit

Gentle Giant is a delightful and rich picture storybook, but some of the structures outlined here might apply to any story about a village or small community faced with a threat from outside. A sense of place and the importance of it are common themes.

3C | The Romans

This unit is based on the Romans and ideas from *Roman Invasion* (*My Story*), by Jim Eldridge, Scholastic, ISBN 978-1-407-10737-0.

Where this unit fits in

Roman Invasion tells the story of Bran, a child prince of the Carvetti tribe who has been captured by the Romans. The defiant young boy is determined to make good use of his time in captivity by absorbing as much information as he can about the Roman soldiers. He aims to take all he has learnt back to his own tribesmen once he has escaped.

The context in which the story is set helps the children to understand why the Romans were so invincible, considering every aspect of their lives, ranging from weaponry and armoury to water and drainage systems. This unit will focus on what Bran learnt about how Roman soldiers fought; drama can really bring this to life.

One of the activities in this unit involves children holding shields. They need to be quite robust because the children will need to hold them up in their battle formations; however, the fronts of the shields will not need to be touched. This provides a good opportunity for children to make their own shields, designing them carefully after gathering information from reference books and the Internet. An activity such as this has natural links between history, literacy, art and technology.

Key learning

Key learning for drama

By the end of this unit, the children will have:

- explored Roman and British tribal weapons through mime;
- choreographed a fight between a Roman soldier and a warrior Briton;
- created battle formations;
- moved from one battle formation to another;
- created a dramatised presentation about Roman soldiers.

Primary Framework for literacy objectives

- Speaking – explain, process or present information, ensuring that items are clearly sequenced, relevant details are included and accounts are ended effectively; explain or give reasons for their views or choices; develop and use specific vocabulary.
- Listening and responding – follow up others' points and show whether they agree or disagree in whole-class discussion.
- Group discussion and interaction – use talk to organise roles and action; actively include and respond to all members of the group.
- Drama – use some drama strategies to explore stories or issues; present events and characters through dialogue to engage the interest of an audience.

Resources

- A cloak.
- Pictures of Roman soldiers and warrior Britons.
- Pictures of the weaponry and armour used by both sides.
- Shields made of tough card (these could be made by children in class).

Steps for teaching and learning

Step 1: Armour used by the Britons

Explain to the children that Bran's tribe has vital armour and weapons that need to be kept in good condition. Although they are heavy, women and children are also used to handling them. Ask them to find a space in the hall where they can stretch out their arms. Tell them that they are going to imagine they are Bran checking the family armour and weapons ready for battle.

Show the children a selection of armour and weapons used by the Britons, and narrate how the children might move and react as they pick up each one. For example:

> First you are going to pick up the axe, so long it would come up to your chin if stood up on its end. You need to pick up the thick wooden handle with two hands, one hand half way down the handle, the other towards the top. Grip it as tightly as you can. The blade of the axe is as thick as a door with a razor-sharp edge. You need to practise swinging the axe, so draw it back, trying hard to keep your balance under the hefty weight, then swing it forward. It is too heavy for you and you stumble forward, just about regaining your balance.

The children mime the narration as you speak it. Children who are less confident may prefer to work in pairs, creating a mirror image of the other during the narration. Move onto describing actions for moving with other weapons such as long spears and swords. Describe them as accurately as possible so that children can later draw a distinction between Roman weaponry and that of the Britons.

Step 2: Close combat

Read the children the part of the story that describes the Romans invading Bran's village. Many citizens and warriors have been killed, but because Bran's family is royal, they have been spared. Bran's older brothers are sent to be slaves who will probably be forced to be gladiators, his sister and his mother are imprisoned in the fort, and he, being a young Carvetti prince, is hostage to the Roman army. There is a very special reason for this. If they are attacked by any of the tribes, the Romans will kill Bran instantly.

Explain to the children that, while he is in captivity, Bran has given himself a very important job; he will spy on the Romans, finding out everything he can about their way of life so that he can take the information back to his tribe once he escapes.

To begin with, repeat the activity that the children did with the Briton's weaponry, this time describing Roman weapons. You might start off by describing a spear:

> Because you are only a child and cannot do much harm, the Romans have allowed you to roam around the camp quite freely. You have wandered through the Roman garrison, and discovered a spear. You reach for the handle, preparing to lift it slowly but finding it almost lifts itself it is so light. It is also quite short. You practise lunging forward with it, noticing how easy it is to move your body from side to side and how close you could get to your opponent.

Once the children have had time to explore Roman armour and weapons, ask them to move into pairs. Provide each pair with a picture of a warrior Briton and a picture of a Roman soldier, with the weapons that they would use for hand-to-hand fighting. Explain that, one night, while Bran was captive to the Romans, they were attacked by a tribe of Britons. He observed the fighting closely so that he could learn how to overcome the Romans later on.

Using pictures and the knowledge they have, the children choreograph a battle scene between a British warrior and a Roman soldier where the Roman must win. The battle should include at least five attacks and at least two of these should be from the Briton.

13

One child will be a Briton, the other a Roman. The first child (in this case, the Briton) calls out their first move. For example: 'A swing of the axe towards the head!'

Calling out the phrase before actually performing the action allows the other child to think about their reaction. The action is performed, without actually making any contact with their partner. The Roman child responds, in this case probably dodging to the side. If the children have considered this carefully, the Roman might counter this with something like, 'A blow to the head!' Once the Roman has performed this action, it is followed by a reaction from the warrior, who may drop further towards the ground. The children continue to work through this until they have a series of fight moves.

Allow the children plenty of time to discuss and practise their moves. They may ask to write them down – let them! Once they have decided on their series of steps, they can then start to rehearse them in order that the movements are more fluid. After a time, invite children to show their 'fight' to the rest of the class.

Eventually, the children will be ready to perform their fight as part of a large battle. This can take place outdoors if the weather is good, but the hall will work just as well. When prompted, all begin to 'fight' at the same time. After a time, only the Roman soldiers will be left standing. When their opponent has been vanquished, the Roman soldier should stand still choosing a victorious pose until all the fighting has finished.

Step 3: Battle formations

Bran learns that Roman success is not just about bravery, it is to do with hard work, discipline and organisation. One day he has the opportunity to watch the soldiers training, moving into different formations that are almost impenetrable. Your class will enjoy creating these. Shields play a very important role in these formations, so this is the time to make them and use them in the drama work.

Begin by asking the children to create the formations from their imaginations, playing a 'Make me a ...' game. Split the class in two, so the numbers in the groups are reasonably high (about 12–15 in each). Assign two officers to each group who will make the final decisions. First, describe what the children are going to 'make':

> The first thing that Bran sees is 'The Tortoise'. You have three minutes to decide what this might look like. If you are not an officer you may only ask questions to the leader, not give suggestions. If you are officers you must be prepared to make a quick decision about how your troops should move.

After the children have had enough discussion time, explain that, when they are asked to move into the formation, there should not be any talking at all. An effective fighting force must be highly disciplined. Then call out, 'Make me a ... *tortoise!*' Repeat the same process for 'The Spear' and 'The Circle'.

Ask each group to watch the other's formation. Each group can ask the other questions about what they have made. For example: 'Why have you chosen to hold your shields above your head?' 'What if someone attacked from this corner?'

Once the children have experimented with their own ideas, you can move on to making the formations as the Romans actually did, this time as a whole class. There are some clear explanations of each formation in Chapter 11 of the book, detailed yet simple to read and understand. For 'The Tortoise', the children form a square where soldiers not only form the sides but also fill the inside. With a shout from the officer, all the soldiers on the outside of the square hold their shields up to eye level, and all those on the inside hold their shields above their head as if to make a roof. They can then move forward together.

For 'The Spear', the shields are held across the chest and the formation takes the shape of an arrowhead. This shape is used to push forward towards the enemy, where it then transforms into 'The Circle'. Soldiers stand in a circle, closing it by holding their shields in front of them so that the sides are almost touching. If any soldier gets killed, another soldier moves into the gap so the circle becomes slightly smaller. This formation allows fighting to be covered on all sides, and there would not have been just one circle but several all along the line.

Once you and the class have worked out how to organise each formation, tell them that they are going to become Roman soldiers who move from one formation to another at the command of an officer. There should be no talking or hesitation, and one formation should move into another with ease. Either you or one of the children can call out the formations.

Step 4: Reporting back to the tribe

The children should now move into groups of four or five. Explain that once the road that passed his and the surrounding villages had been built, Bran was allowed to return to his village and was reunited with some members of his family. The first thing they do is share all the knowledge they have learnt about the Romans since they have been in captivity.

Ask each group to sit in a circle and place a shield in the centre of each. Each child takes a turn to hold the shield, describing one thing they have learnt about the Romans, then passes it to the next child. After the shield has passed all around the circle once, it can then be placed in the middle and anyone can take a turn to lift the shield and discuss what has been learned.

Once the children have pooled their knowledge, explain to them that they will now share everything they have learned with the rest of the tribe. The information needs to be as clear as possible, so much of the explanation will need to be shown physically by enacting the way the Romans fought and showing how a formation might look.

They may also include information they have learnt through other lessons about the Romans. Give the children creative restrictions; the presentation should have no more than five points and each child should make at least one verbal contribution as well as physical.

Although everyone will speak at some point, the group may choose to have a main presenter who will introduce each part. This activity will provide you with a general picture of what children have learnt and understood about the Romans. While each group presents their knowledge, the rest of the class take roles as members of the tribe, asking questions to explore how the Roman threat might be overcome. From their roles, the children can make suggestions about how they might adapt their weaponry, armour and tactics to take account of what they have learned.

Guidance for assessment

Any assessment of this work will be related back to the Key learning for drama, which stated that by the end of this unit the children will have:

- worked individually to explore Roman and British tribal weapons through mime – *how successfully can the children respond through their bodies?*
- worked in pairs to choreograph a fight between a Roman soldier and a warrior Briton – *to what extent have the children transferred their knowledge about weapons and armour to their drama? Do the children improve and adapt their performance through rehearsal?*
- worked in large groups to create battle formations.
- worked with the class to move from one battle formation to another – *are the children able to use good control and show confidence when working as part of a large group?*
- worked as a group to create a presentation about Roman soldiers – *how well do the presentations illustrate children's knowledge of Roman Britain? How well organised is each presentation? Is everyone confident in their role?*

Adapting this unit

Work on the Romans in Britain may be in your plans for any year group in the 7–11 age range. Older children will be expected to infer more from a range of historical sources and ask more questions about their validity, so you might expect their research to play a greater part in the early stages of this work. You will also expect a greater degree of control and planning in the fight arranging. You might extend the unit by going on to look at the story of Boudicca and the Iceni uprising. The basic structure for researching and choreographing a fight could also be adapted for other history work.

3F   *Dr Xargle's Book of Earthlets*

This unit is based on *Dr Xargle's Book of Earthlets*, by Jeanne Willis and Tony Ross, Andersen Press Paperback Picture Books, ISBN 978-1-842-70067-9.

Where this unit fits in

Dr Xargle's Book of Earthlets is a highly amusing read that appeals to children of all ages. In its pages we watch a group of alien students come down on a visit to Earth, drawing strange conclusions about how ordinary objects from Earth are used. Things humans take for granted are given completely different names; reasons why humans do things are entirely misinterpreted.

In this unit, your class will take the role of aliens, imagining that they are on a study trip to their own classroom. They will use earthling technology (laptop computers linked to the Internet) to investigate whether they can send messages on it through space. This will give the children an opportunity to collect their 'discoveries' in an interesting way.

Linking with another school can provide rich opportunities for sharing ideas and experiences. If another school could go on an Earthlet expedition to their classroom, the two (or more) schools could communicate what they had found through email, almost as if there are separate alien missions going on simultaneously. This gives the children the sense of a real and imaginary audience.

Key learning

Key learning for drama

By the end of this unit, the children will have:

- worked imaginatively in pairs and groups to describe familiar objects in unusual ways;
- worked in role to gather information to be sent to an imaginary source;
- used drama as a stimulus to see ordinary things in a different way;
- created films, collected and annotated photographs, made notes and word-processing to communicate their 'Earthling discoveries'.

Primary Framework for literacy objectives

- Speaking – develop and use specific vocabulary in different contexts; identify the presentational features used to communicate the main points in a broadcast.
- Group discussion and interaction – use talk to organise roles and action; actively include and respond to all members of the group.
- Drama – use some drama strategies to explore stories and issues; present events and characters through dialogue to engage the interest of an audience.
- Creating and shaping texts – write non-narrative texts using structures of different text-types: select and use a range of technical and descriptive vocabulary; use layout, format graphics and illustrations for different purposes.

Resources

- Paired access to laptops or PCs.
- A simple presentational program (such as Textease or Microsoft PowerPoint) where the children will import all the information (such as movie or sound clips, photographs and text) onto one page, organise and present it.

- Examples of websites and instructional texts to help children make choices about how to present several blocks of information on the same screen.
- Digital cameras – those that take pictures and those that take video (in many cases this might be on the same camera).
- Recording equipment would also be useful, such as Dictaphones that can be plugged into a USB port.
- A digital microscope – all English primary schools were sent one of these a few years ago and they can be another good way of seeing ordinary and everyday things in new ways.
- Sometimes it will be necessary to work in the classroom so the 'aliens' can collect some good evidence to send back to their planet; sometimes it will be better to work in the hall, for example when the aliens hold their 'summit meetings'.
- A variety of sports equipment, e.g. rugby balls, footballs, hockey sticks, javelins, etc. There should be enough of these to share one between two.

Steps for teaching and learning

Step 1: Seeing things in new ways

One of the things that the children will find most challenging is to see their classroom and their world with completely new eyes. When they work through the alien activities, they will need to playfully forget their human view of things.

A good first step for the children is to try playing an alien barrier game. Ask the children to split into pairs. Explain that they are going to sit back to back and imagine that one of them is speaking from a control centre on another planet, whilst the other is describing a new piece of equipment they have discovered on Earth. In this case, the only form of communication they can use is sound, not pictures, so the verbal description will need to be very clear. The child who has the object must never give the Earthly name for it, and the person listening must find out about it by asking questions and sketch what they think it might look like, based on the description.

21

After a time, tell the children they both have the job of working out what humans use the item for and what they should call it. They should still have their backs to each other to continue the idea that communication is only being maintained through sound.

After this, ask all your 'aliens' to gather in a circle as if they are having a summit meeting back at their own planet. They are going to present their discoveries to the rest of the class. All are keen to make their discovery sound the most exciting and profound, and when each of them is presented, encourage children to ask questions afterwards to fine-tune the details about each 'device' and how it should be used.

The children will have great fun doing this because they will be describing ordinary objects in a very unfamiliar way. It will challenge children to describe things in unusual ways which is a great way to enrich children's language. They will also enjoy the sense of audience in the task.

Step 2: Collecting evidence

Now move the pairs into fours and give each group a digital camera. They need to take good photographs of their object and import the photographs onto a page on their computer. Once they have done this, they will then need to add a sound file to describe what they have found. Many laptops have inbuilt microphones, or you may have simple microphones that you can plug into a USB port.

Each child in the group must have a specific role. Ask the children to give themselves a number, one, two, three or four. Ones are going to be interviewers; twos are going to be the explorer who actually found it, saying where it was discovered and giving a description of the item; threes and fours are going to be the scientists who have studied in the alien laboratory to work out what it might have been used for.

The children will need to practise presenting and recording. Listening to their first recording will be really useful for them – they will be able to hear instantly where there is too much of a pause, where the talking isn't immediate or interesting enough, and where people are speaking too slowly or too quickly. Model for the children how they can use notes to help them when they are communicating their ideas and, if you feel it is appropriate, give them a simple frame that might help them to structure their talk. Once this has been completed, they have the first piece of information on their explanatory text.

Step 3: Life in school

Your class of aliens can then investigate the wider concept of school itself. Again, they will find this task amusing as they will have to view their everyday objects and activities in school in a completely different light.

Ask the children to stay in their groups of four. One child will be director and camera person, the other three will create four still images of typical school life. What is important about this is that, although the children are creating still images, they should not look like holiday snapshots. Aliens taking photographs of humans would be doing so in secret, so none of the children will be looking at the camera, and each still image should look as if they are in the middle of doing something active and engaging.

The only thing that you need to stipulate here is that the four images need to show four different aspects of school life. Unlike in other photographic or film work, the children do not have to worry too much about what is in the background (unless it is from a compositional point of view) because everything to do with school will provide good evidence for the aliens to explore and investigate.

Again, these images need to be downloaded onto the computer. Eventually, the children will annotate these images, but before they do, their thinking can be challenged through further role play.

23

Step 4: Sharing the images

Now tell the children that they are going to reform their tableaux for the rest of the class to see. The idea is that there is going to be another alien summit where the fourth alien who is not part of the tableau will present a set of four full-sized 3D images to the other aliens (the children will just move from one tableau to another). The group must decide what Alien Four must do to signal the change from one tableau to another (it could be an imaginary click of a mouse, or a sweep of hand in the air) and Child Four will be giving an explanation of what he or she thinks is happening in each image.

Give the children thinking and discussion time so they can decide as a group what is being shown in each image. For example, aliens might think that children are using their pens to drill into their desks rather than hold them. They might think that when they put their hands up it is a type of exercise or a way of keeping warm. Suggest a couple of these ideas to the children before they start their work – they will have something to aim for and will enjoy the opportunity to amuse and entertain the rest of the class.

As each group takes a turn at presenting the four tableaux, this can be filmed by other groups – they can take turns at filming for each different presentation. This will bring the idea of 'community' into the project, so that they are also including the work of other aliens in their page of discovery.

If the children do have the chance to film these, ask them to choose their favourite one clip to avoid there being too much information on the screen. Once the children have created this presentation, they will have plenty of ideas to take back to their ICT work so that each picture can be annotated with details of what the humans are actually doing in each picture.

Step 5: Playing with language

One of the things that children may enjoy most about this project is writing alien instructions. The next topic for the aliens to investigate is sport. Ask each group to choose an activity from PE that uses apparatus or equipment, such as football.

As a group, they must explain to the other aliens how this activity works, but must replace the usual technical language with words that the aliens use. For example, the aliens may describe a football as a 'toe globe'. They may describe a kick as a 'leg swish'. This is not about creating nonsense words in a made-up language (as you can show them from the original book), it is more to do with threading together other ordinary words to make new phrases and terminology.

Each group should make up a set of four instructions that they will demonstrate in steps to the rest of the group. Each of the other groups will be given the same apparatus so that they can follow the instructions and try it out themselves. They will then be allowed to ask questions afterwards.

Finally, this instructional activity can be filmed and you may decide that you would like the children to write the accompanying instructions to add onto the page; depending on the facilities that your computers have for editing, they may be able to add these over the top of the image.

What the children will have created in simple steps is a whole page of information about a visit to Earth which includes different types of text; explanatory and instructional within a fictional context. Although on one page, the selection of texts the children have used will have been presented in a variety of ways, and throughout they will have been thinking about audience, knowing that the information they collect will need to be very clear and easy to understand.

As the activities have progressed, the children will have had to use their imagination and find new ways of using the language that they use every day. They will have noticed the small details in ordinary things that, through familiarity, people learn to forget.

Step 6: How do the aliens see us?

Although this book is very playful, this work can also present opportunities for children to suggest some things that might concern the aliens about the way humans live and behave. What things about life in school do they think could be made better? Do they, for example, think children get enough exercise? If you extend the activities by working outdoors, are there things that concern or mystify them about the school grounds, or perhaps the traffic around the school and the dangers it presents to children? From the perspective of the aliens, children have a safe place from which they can not only make playful and funny suggestions, but perhaps also make some more serious points about things that concern them and that they would like to see change.

Guidance on assessment

Any assessment of this work will be related back to the Key learning for drama, which stated that by the end of this unit the children will have:

* worked imaginatively in pairs and groups to describe familiar objects in unusual ways – *as the children progress through the activities, how well are they able to describe items and situations without using their familiar names?*
* worked in role to gather information to be sent to an imaginary source – *how successfully do the children stay in role and to what extent is this used to improve the quality of the information gathered? How well do the children structure their verbal presentations? Do all children have a role in their groups and do they work as successfully when the roles are changed?*
* created films, collected and annotated photographs, made notes and word-processing to communicate their 'Earthling discoveries' – *to what extent do the children transfer the powerful language they used in drama to their written presentations?*

Adapting this unit

Children across the 7–11 age range will enjoy this work. If you are going to adapt it for older children, you will probably expect them to take more control over the ICT work. They will also need to be more adventurous in their use of language, and you may want to make more of Step 6 ('How do the aliens see us?') to explore some deeper issues about their lives in school and beyond.

3P All about our town

Where this unit fits in

This unit offers an opportunity to work with your local community to create a performance that explores and celebrates what is unique about the history and culture of your area. What do they like about living in this place? How did it come to be like it is? Who has lived here before them? How might it change in the future? Thinking about and researching these questions together will challenge you and your class to devise imaginative ways of staging what you have learned.

Although we have put this unit in the performance strand, the children will need to do plenty of research about the history and geography of their local area, which might readily form part of a larger piece of work taking in a number of subjects and areas. The unit includes opportunities to work with family, friends and members of the wider community to collect stories and memories, likes and dislikes, and hopes for the area they live in. The eventual performance will also involve children's ideas for designing and making sets, composing music and creating dance.

Key learning

Key learning for drama

By the end of this unit, the children will have:

- collaborated in groups to research and dramatise some of the people and events in their local area;
- made suggestions for how their own and others' work can be improved;
- rehearsed and refined their work for performance to an audience;
- contributed to the design and staging decisions for the eventual performance;
- taken part in a performance for an invited audience.

Primary Framework for literacy objectives

- Group discussion and interaction – use talk to organise roles and action; actively include and respond to all members of the group.
- Drama – present events and characters through dialogue to engage the interest of an audience; use some drama strategies to explore stories or issues; identify and discuss qualities of others' performances, including gesture, action and costume.

Resources

- The 'community post box' described in Step 1 need be no more than a cardboard box with a slot cut in the top, but if someone is prepared to make something more elaborate and substantial it can help to give the project a higher profile and sense of importance.
- Simple video cameras and voice recorders can be very useful for recording people's stories and memories in Steps 1 and 2.
- As you will see in Step 7, you may decide to use a data projector in your eventual performance, perhaps using a simple cloth as a screen.

Steps for teaching and learning

Step 1: The community post box

It will be important to start sharing your plans for this unit at an early stage, probably some months before the eventual performance. Work with the children to compose a letter to parents and other members of the community asking them for thoughts, memories and stories about the area. Who has lived here for a long time? What can they remember about this place in the past? Who has joined the community more recently? Where have they come from? What was it like to move here?

Ask for as many responses as possible to be put in a 'community post box' near the school reception. Responses can be written, might include photographs that people are willing to share, perhaps even sound or video recordings. Many schools now have access to inexpensive video cameras that could be set up for people to come in and record anecdotes and memories.

If you have done this kind of project before, you will know very well that just leaving the post box out and hoping for the best is very unlikely to work. You will need to be tenacious, even to the point of being tiresome, in encouraging parents and other community members to come and contribute. Talk to parents before and after school, visit local shops, pubs and clubs, and ask as many people as possible. If you are not comfortable talking to people in this way, find the people on your staff who are and take them with you.

Step 2: Who shall they talk to?

Once the post box has been out for long enough to collect a good number of contributions, you can begin to sift through it with the class to see what stories, thoughts and memories interest them most. Clearly you will need to be sensitively selective to avoid contributions that could upset or offend sections of the community.

As you look through the contributions with your class, you will see which ones interest, excite and amuse them. Even at this early stage, you can begin thinking about which stories, memories and anecdotes might be good to include and how you might dramatise and stage them. You will also start to form ideas about who you might like to invite into school to talk about their knowledge, memories and experiences of living in the community. They may be people who have lived in the area for a long time and have seen lots of changes; they may be people who have done particular jobs in the community (shopkeepers, religious leaders, police officers, etc.); or they may be people who are quite new to the area and have chosen to live here for particular reasons. Once you have decided who you might like to invite, plan carefully for the visits, getting the children to think about what questions they will ask and how they will record the answers – video and sound recording can be really useful here.

Step 3: Researching the local history

Talking to people in the community can be a great way of getting some insight into the history of any place. Many communities have local history societies or individuals who have considerable knowledge. Your local library will also be very helpful and many have access to archives of old photographs and other documents, many of which have been digitised and are available online. Your school may also have a teacher, teaching assistant or other member of staff who knows the local area and its history well and would be keen to help. All these sources will help you and your class build up a picture of your community's particular history.

Step 4: Working in groups to begin devising

As you have been exploring the story of your community together, there will be particular incidents, anecdotes and photographs that will have appealed to the children. Having divided them into groups of three or four, ask each group to choose one idea and prepare it to present to the rest of the class. It might be a story that an older member of the community told about getting into trouble at school, it might be a photograph of an event or celebration, or it might be the fact that the town began as an Anglo-Saxon settlement by the river. Starting from these, ask each group to devise a short scene (no more than a minute or two at this stage) that brings the story, picture or history to life. To do this, children will need to imagine much of the detail, and this can be explored further when their work is presented for the rest of the class. As each group's work is performed, ask the others to comment. Do they think the performers used the right kind of language? Was it clear what had happened? How did the short performances make the children feel? How could they be developed and improved?

Step 5: From improvising to scripting and refining

As each group is encouraged to develop and extend their work, they can begin to write down who says what. They are often introduced to some of the conventions of script-writing at this stage and this can be a good way of encouraging them to be more deliberate in what they say. You may want to develop their scripts as part of a writing lesson but, if you do, remind them that their words are written to be performed and that they need to keep trying them out to see how they sound and feel. Again, the process of writing, performing and refining can be helped by groups sharing their work with the rest of the class as it develops. Working like this, you will soon find that you have the core of a script around which you can build your final performance. Obviously you will need to use your own judgement about how much you need to intervene to refine and develop the children's work, but it is important that the children feel the script is the result of their own work, rather than something their teacher has written for them.

Step 6: Developing an overall structure

So far you will have a number of short scenes developed by the groups. You may extend the range of stories and events you include by asking each group to devise a second scene in the same way – this will give you a dozen or so which can form the core of your eventual performance. Now you can begin to talk about how the scenes might be joined together to make a complete performance. How will they arrange them? Chronologically so the story of their town is told in order? Reverse chronologically so they gradually go back in time? Is there a theme or an object that might link all the scenes together in another way – perhaps an idea like the old church clock looking down and seeing changes over time? Do they need to add extra scenes at the beginning or end so that it is clear to the audience what is happening? Where might they include music, song and dance? Again, involving the children in as much of this process as possible will help them to take genuine pride in what they have created that will be reflected in their eventual performance.

Step 7: Designing and staging

Where will your performance be staged? Many take place in the school hall and that would be great, but this may also be a good opportunity to think of other places in and around your community. If you are going to 'tour' a piece of work in this way, then the design needs to be simple, clear and easy to move. What about using projection, perhaps of some of the old photographs that stimulated the work, pictures of locations where things happened, perhaps with children posing there in costume? What sort of costumes are needed? Who can help? As you explore these questions together, you will generate genuine excitement about your performance, not just with children but also among their parents and the wider community.

Step 8: Getting ready to perform

As we stress throughout these performance units, if you expect high standards from the children they will rise to them. Don't be afraid to be insistent about clarity and precision, always bearing in mind that a short performance of high quality is much preferable to a longer one that has your audience wondering when it will end. Because they have been involved in the devising and development of this project from the start, the performance can have a real sense of shared celebration for the children, the school and the community it serves.

Guidance on assessment

Any assessment of this work will be related back to the Key learning for drama, which stated that by the end of this unit the children will have:

- collaborated in groups to research and dramatise some of the people and events in their local area – *how successful are they in translating what they have seen, read and heard into dramatic action?*
- made suggestions for how their own and others' work can be improved – *who contributes ideas for how others' work can be improved and developed? How well do they respond to suggestions and incorporate them into their developing work?*
- rehearsed and refined their work for performance to an audience – *do they show an awareness of audience as their work develops?*
- contributed to the design and staging decisions for the eventual performance – *who makes imaginative and practical suggestions?*
- taken part in a performance for an invited audience – *how is the performance received by parents and the community? Which children have enjoyed it and performed well?*

Adapting this unit

Although we have chosen to place this unit in Year 3, the structure it uses could be used right across the primary age range. Collecting and exploring material and working together to find imaginative and inventive ways of presenting it will be a terrific challenge for all of your classes and, particularly if you work in a small school, it might be a very good project to undertake with more than one class or year group working together.

Theseus and the Minotaur

This unit is based on *Theseus and the Minotaur*.

Where this unit fits in

The King of Athens has been forced to make a terrible agreement with King Minos, ruler of Crete. Every year, six Athenian men and six Athenian women are chosen to travel to the Island of Crete to be fed to the hideous Minotaur – a strange beast who is half man and half bull and lives in a maze beneath the palace. But one year Theseus, Prince of Athens, decides that he wants to be one of the 12, vowing to defeat the Minotaur. With great reluctance, the King agrees, insisting that Theseus should fly a black sail on his departure but should change the sail to white if he returns. His father will know that if he sees the ship return with a black sail, Theseus is dead.

King Minos of Crete has a beautiful daughter called Ariadne who falls in love with Theseus the instant she sees him arrive on the island. Knowing of his intent, she decides to help, secretly presenting him with a ball of thread and a dagger: the thread to help him to find his way out of the labyrinth, the dagger to slay the beast. Theseus promises that he will take Ariadne away with him if he succeeds.

Although Theseus defeats the Minotaur, his conduct as a hero is debatable. Despite his promise to Ariadne, he stops at another island on the way back to Athens and leaves her there on the shore. He also 'forgets' to change the sail from black to white, so that his Father, overcome with grief, throws himself off the cliff where he waited in hope of his son's safe return.

In this literacy-based unit, the activities lead to a possible written outcome: a description of the journey through the maze told from Theseus' point of view.

This is an ancient story that can tell us a great deal about ancient Greek and Minoan society, and would clearly connect with history work on the Greeks, but could also be done as a stand-alone unit.

Key learning

Key learning for drama

By the end of this unit, the children will have:

* answered questions in role about mysterious objects, starting to piece them together to make a story;
* worked in pairs to enact a conversation between two characters, based on a picture;
* worked in groups to create a soundscape for their classmates;
* taken a partner on a guided tour, using written prompts to help them to describe the labyrinth.

Primary Framework for literacy objectives

* Speaking – tell stories effectively and convey detailed information coherently for listeners.
* Group discussion and interaction – take different roles in groups and use the language appropriate to them, including the roles of leader, reporter, scribe and mentor.
* Drama – create roles showing how behaviour can be interpreted from different viewpoints; develop scripts based on improvisation; comment constructively on plays and performances, discussing effects and how they are achieved.

Resources

- A ball of thread.
- A toy/stage dagger.
- A large piece of black cloth.
- A still or moving image of water to project (optional).
- An overhead projector or data projector (optional).

Steps for teaching and learning

Step 1: Questioning the keeper of secrets

Before the children know anything about the story, create a sense of mystery and adventure as soon as they walk in the room. Have the sound of the sea playing in the background and, if possible, an image of water projected onto the floor. In the middle of the room place a piece of black cloth, an unravelled thread and a dagger. Do not give any explanation about these items; at this stage you are just encouraging children to be curious about what they see.

Give each child a few adhesive notes and a pencil. Ask them to write down as many questions as possible about the scene. Encourage them not to worry about spelling and stress that no question is too ordinary or too ridiculous. There should be one question per note – they can write as many as they want, but give them a time limit of no more than two minutes.

Ask the children to spread their notes on and around the scene.

The children now move into pairs. Ask them to give themselves a number: one or two. Number ones are the keeper of the secrets. Number twos ask questions that their partner will answer, pretending that they know everything there is to know about the setting and the story. As they talk, they should move around the room, number twos looking for different questions that have been arranged around the scene, but also thinking of any other questions that could be drawn out of number one's response. It is important that number ones know that there is no wrong here and they can respond in any way they like. If they want to respond as themselves telling the story they can, if they want to experiment with creating a storyteller character who answers the questions, they can do that too. It will help the children if you model the exercise for them before they start – this will not only give them a benchmark but also a default response; if they get stuck and don't know what to say, they can start off with their teacher's idea.

Give this question and answer session about two to three minutes, then ask the children to swap. Number twos can continue the story in the same style if they wish, or they can respond in a completely different way. Walk around and listen in to the children's talk, so you can be ready to pick out some examples when the activity has finished.

Step 2: Using an image from the story

The children will have generated some interesting ideas about the role of the sea and the objects in the story. Now you can introduce them to another 'clue'. One of the key moments in the legend is when Theseus asks his father to allow him to go to face the Minotaur. His father is appalled by the idea and begs his son not to go. Because this is such a dramatic moment, storybooks usually have a very striking image to accompany the text (there are also plenty of images to be found on the Internet). The image often shows the father on his knees to his son, pleading with him not to go; an interesting juxtaposition of power.

Show this or a similar image to the children, again without any explanation of the story. Ask the children to remain in their pairs and look at the picture closely. Give them one minute to discuss what could be happening in the scene, then stop them. They then need to find a space and improvise the conversation and action that could be taking place in this scene. There are usually some very interesting responses. Those children who look very closely might notice that the clothes of the person kneeling down are more elaborate than the person who is standing. Sometimes the children assume that the conversation taking place is between two women because the characters are wearing robes. As the children are acting out their ideas, walk around, listen and watch. It may be necessary to stop them and offer reminders about how to use the space effectively, or how to make the actions positive and clear. It may be appropriate to challenge or guide them if you are not happy with their responses. When they have had time to explore and develop their ideas, then encourage them to refine them by condensing the dialogue to only ten words. This restriction focuses the children and helps them to think more creatively.

Take time to watch and comment on some of the examples. By this point the children will be intrigued to know the story that you are holding back from them, so it is time to tell it!

Step 3: Theseus meets the Minotaur

After you have finished telling or reading the children the story, explain that it is rarely told from Theseus' point of view and there is much debate about how heroic he actually was. Tell the children that they are going to have the opportunity to decide what sort of a character Theseus was, and to tell the most exciting parts of the story in his words.

The first part of the story that they are going to tell is how it felt to walk through the corridors of the pitch-black labyrinth. In order to create this, the children move into groups and create soundscapes of the labyrinth for their classmates using only their voices and bodies to make the sounds.

To begin with, ask the class to form a large circle and discuss the sorts of sounds that might be heard. These might include scuttling insects; the distant footsteps of the Minotaur stopping, starting, slowly moving closer; the intermittent whimpering of a lost Athenian; the crunching of human bones underfoot. Show the children how moments of silence, followed by something as simple as a quick scratching noise on the floor or the sound of a heavy breath, can heighten suspense and tension. Tell the children that you expect their soundscape to include these things:

- gentle individual sounds;
- at least three pauses which are moments of absolute silence;
- a selection of layered sounds that children make at the same time;
- no more than three sudden unexpected noises.

The impact of a soundscape is really dependent on where the performers place the audience and how they interact with them. For example, they might choose to turn the lights off and have all their audience sitting in the middle of the room with their eyes closed. When they perform the different sounds from the labyrinth they might move in and out of the audience or even behind them. When they make breathing sounds they might lean in to the tops of their heads, or they might tap their audience gently on the back as they pass by. Alternatively, the performers could choose to spread themselves around the room, and have the audience walking in and around them, just as Theseus would as he journeyed through the twists and turns of the labyrinth.

Before the children perform their soundscape, make sure you have listened to and watched each group. Ensure that each group is clear about where to start and finish and that they all know when to take their turn.

When the children have experienced being the audience of the soundscape, they will be inspired and excited by the impact that it has had. They will be ready to capture their ideas so they can be threaded together into a final piece of writing.

Step 4: Word labyrinth

Make sure the children have access to plenty of scrap paper and thick
marker pens. They are going to create a carpet of words that they will
spread across the hall describing Theseus' experiences in the
labyrinth. Each piece of paper should include only one idea, which
could be a word, a phrase or a few sentences about the same element.
For example, one Year 4 child we worked with wrote:

> I can feel the hot breath of the Minotaur on the back of my neck.
> My body is tense.

Another child wrote:

> I can feel the ground shaking under my feet. In the distance there
> is the sound of heavy footsteps, sometimes fast, sometimes slow.

Sometimes the children might only write a few words:

> Bones rolling underfoot.

Step 5: Walking the labyrinth

Using the method of 'guided tour' can help the children to begin
threading their phrases together to make a story. Working in pairs,
the children take turns to lead each other through the 'word
labyrinth'. The child who is led has their eyes closed while their
partner leads them and narrates the journey by using the language
that has been spread on the floor. For example:

> Be careful here, there are bones scattered across the floor and it is
> easy to lose your footing, they roll under your feet. Stop! We must
> change direction, I can hear the heavy thud of the Minotaur's
> feet and it seems to be coming closer!

Again, it is very helpful if you model this process for the children
before they start.

Once the children have got to the point where they are using their phrases to prompt their ideas for a description, you can model how this can be developed into a piece of extended writing. Obviously you will draw on the features and structures of text that you will have been studying in other literacy lessons, but you will also find the word labyrinth a useful and powerful tool of reference. Not only will you be teaching the children how to structure their work, but also how to use the details from the experiences to enrich their writing.

Guidance for assessment

Any assessment of this work will be related back to the Key learning for drama, which stated that by the end of this unit, the children will have:

- answered questions in role about mysterious objects, starting to piece them together to make a story – *are the children able to respond in role and give positive, convincing responses? If they pause to think about an answer, can they still maintain their role and think of useful phrases to fill the pauses?*
- worked in pairs to act out a conversation between two characters, based on a picture – *do the children draw on evidence from the picture to enhance the action? Do they display an awareness of audience in the way that they choose to present the conversation, i.e. do they think about the way they are facing or whether one character is blocking another?*
- worked in groups to create a soundscape for their classmates – *how disciplined are the children when they are performing the soundscape? Are they able to maintain a sense of suspense through silence as well as sound? Are they aware of pace?*
- taken a partner on a guided tour, using written prompts to help them to describe the labyrinth – *are the children aware of the importance of staying in role to create an exciting atmosphere for their partner? Are they able to say the words they read with effect? How dramatically do they express the experience of walking through the labyrinth?*

Adapting this unit

We have used the basic structure of this work successfully across the 7–11 age range. You can adapt it and apply it to many other stories where you want the children to experience a sense of tension and suspense.

Change in the environment

Where this unit fits in

The British Isles have a great many disused railway lines and a quick look at an Ordnance Survey map of your local area may well show one quite near to your school. Many are abandoned and inaccessible; others may be used as walks, cycle tracks and nature reserves. The idea for this unit came from proposals to re-open a disused railway near the Warwickshire town of Southam so that it could be used to transport freight for a local cement company. It is a particularly good environmental issue to use because all the possible uses of the railway which the children explore have strong environmental cases, so the unit offers them some genuine, thought-provoking dilemmas. If you cannot adapt it for your own local area, then you might base this unit on OS Explorer sheet 222 (Rugby and Daventry). The unit is outlined here as if you were working locally, but can readily be adapted if not. As with all the units, we give some guidance on doing this at the end.

This unit connects with the humanities curriculum, in particular work on the local area and the theme of environmental change. If you choose a local railway line, then there may also be very strong connections with the performance unit for Year 4, 'All about our town'. It could easily form part of a wider project that could involve fieldwork, perhaps including interviews with members of the local community, research from the Internet and other sources, and presentations orally, in writing and using ICT.

Key learning

Key learning for drama

By the end of this unit, the children will have:

- taken roles as experts in marketing and public relations and responded to their teacher in role;
- worked in their expert roles to prepare and present a case;
- created a still–move–still structure to explore reactions in the local community;
- worked in a second role as members of the local community;
- reflected on a number of issues and possibilities, and physically represented some of the tensions between them.

Primary Framework for literacy objectives

- Speaking – offer reasons and evidence for their views, considering alternative opinions; respond appropriately to the contributions of others in the light of differing viewpoints.
- Listening – listen to a speaker, make notes on the talk and use notes to develop a role play.
- Group discussion and interaction – take different roles in groups and use the language appropriate to them, including the roles of leader, reporter, scribe and mentor.
- Drama – use time, resources and group members efficiently by distributing tasks, checking progress and making back-up plans.
- Creating and shaping texts – summarise and shape material and ideas from different sources to write convincing and informative non-narrative texts.

Resources

- An Ordnance Survey map of the area you have chosen to study.
- Plenty of photographs and video of the area chosen, contemporary and, if possible, archive.
- Access to the local library and Internet for research.

Steps for teaching and learning

Step 1: Establishing the background

Talk to the children about what they know about a local disused railway line. Who has been for a walk or ridden their bike along one? What sorts of things do they see there? What sorts of plants and animals are there? This activity will be greatly enhanced if you write to parents and encourage them to visit the local railway with their children. You can also encourage children to talk to friends and family about the railway. How do they use it? What do they remember about it? Can anyone remember it when it was still open? It will also help if you have the chance to visit yourself and take plenty of pictures and video to share with children and encourage discussion. Sites such as Google Maps will also allow you to explore maps and aerial photographs of the area in considerable detail.

The children can also conduct some research about the railway and its history. There may well be archive photographs and other records in the local library and on the Internet that allow them to find out details such as when it was built, what it was used for and when it closed.

Rather than ask the children to present their findings and ideas just orally or in writing, get them to work in groups to prepare tableaux or short scenes that show what they have learned about their railway and its history.

Step 2: Meeting the company

Explain to the children that they are going to be in role as experts who have been called in by a local company to help them develop plans for the railway and present them to the local community. Talk about where they think the headquarters of the company might be and what it might be like. At this point you begin to move away from reality and create a fiction together, so you can go with the children's ideas. What sort of building do they think it might be?

Where would they go when they arrived there? What sort of room might the experts meet in? The children will have plenty of ideas about this and, when we have worked with them, have usually suggested a 'boardroom' style of meeting. Take some time to set up the classroom in this way, moving desks and chairs to make a large open table that can seat everyone around it. It may also be worth adding details such as pads of paper, pens and pencils at each place, perhaps bottles of water on the tables – all this can help the children feel in role.

Take the role of the company representative and, addressing the children in role, thank them for coming and explain the purpose of the meeting. Your company is exploring a possible plan to re-open a railway line to transport goods. You have looked into it very carefully and concluded that railway transport would not only be economically good, it would also be good for the environment because it would keep so many lorries off the roads. Your only problem is that the old railway line has become popular with walkers, cyclists and naturalists, so you fear it may be difficult to convince local communities that re-opening it is a good idea. This is where you need their help.

Keeping in role, ask what the main 'selling points' of the idea might be? How might they begin to convince the local community? This initial discussion need not be very long; probably no more than ten minutes or so. But it is important that the children stay in role and contribute as experts.

Step 3: Making the case

Out of role, talk to the children about how they might present a good case for re-opening the railway. What are the advantages of using this kind of transport? Are there any disadvantages? How might these be overcome?

Combining work from humanities, writing and drama lessons, the children present the case for re-opening the railway in the most effective and imaginative ways that they can. This might involve creating posters and leaflets using ICT, perhaps making ICT-based presentations or creating work that could be part of a website all about the proposals. By asking the children to work as if they were expert consultants called in by the company, you give them a kind of professional detachment from the issue that will prove very useful later in the unit. It is worth stressing that, although they are preparing their work as if it were for the company, you do not expect them to stay 'in role' all the time they are doing it. Once everything is done, however, you will probably want to set up a second meeting with the company representative at which the experts present their work. During this meeting both you and the children will stay in your respective roles. Your role will allow you to ask some searching questions about the case they have presented, but also to accept their expertise in the matter. Done with commitment, this kind of role playing can be very powerful.

Step 4: Rumours in the local community

Look again at the map of the local area and track the course of the railway. If the line does re-open, who might be affected by it? What views about it do they think other people might have?

Ask the children to create tableaux that depict different locations on the map: they may be local shops, pubs, farms, or perhaps the old railway line itself. The tableaux will immediately give some clues as to how people might be feeling when they hear about plans for their railway, and this can be extended by developing them into a still–move–still. Ask the children to hold one still, bring it alive for a few moments, and then hold a second still. In these fragments of conversation, they can convey a very clear idea about how the plans for the railway are received. You may well get a range of reactions but, even though the children worked on the case for it themselves, they will almost certainly understand that there will be considerable resistance to it in the local area. People are likely to be concerned about the noise, the disruption while it is built and the loss of a local amenity. Having the opportunity to present both sides of the argument in this way is both challenging and enjoyable.

Step 5: A public meeting

Tell the children that the company who want to re-open the railway have decided to hold a public meeting to discuss their plans with the local community. Where do the children think the meeting might be held? How might the room be set up? Who would speak first? From where?

Using all their ideas, set up a space (probably the hall) to represent the public meeting. They are very likely to decide on an arrangement of rows of chairs facing the front. You will probably want a screen and projector to show their ICT presentations, and some tables and boards to display the rest of their work.

Once the room is set up, tell the children that they are going to come into the space as if they were the local residents coming to the meeting. As they move in and start looking around, call 'Freeze' every few moments, asking the children to hold a still and think about how the residents might be feeling. As they hold each still, you can also feed back on what you see: 'Some people seem very unsure and unhappy about the idea', etc. Then take the role of the company representative and ask everyone to take their seats so the meeting can begin.

As the company representative you will speak to the whole meeting. Through your role, outline the plans and refer to the materials the children produced in their earlier work. If you come across as a little nervous and uncertain about the plans, children will quickly pick up on this and start asking some very difficult questions from their roles as local residents. You may be surprised by how quickly the meeting becomes heated and starts to feel very real! Always remember that you can step out of role and 'freeze' the meeting at any point to talk with the class about how it is going.

The meeting will generate many more possibilities for children to write in role – this time as local residents who want to express their views about the plan. They can write letters and emails, design posters and newsletters to make their case.

Step 6: An alternative plan (optional)

At this stage you can introduce a third option. Tell the children that a rival plan has emerged to open the railway up as a cycle path to form part of a national cycling network. If you wish to, you can spend further time looking at the case for this and presenting it in much the same way as you did the case for re-opening the railway.

Step 7: Taking a stand

By now, the children will have explored two or three options in some detail. Should the railway be left undisturbed, re-opened for freight, or perhaps used as part of the national cycle network? Write the two (or three) options on large sheets of paper and place them a good distance apart on the hall floor. Now ask children to 'take a stand'. They do not have to settle completely on one option, but may also stand in the spaces between them to show where the balance of their views lie. From these stances, ask the children to be ready to speak a few words when you tap them on the shoulder, then move among them hearing their responses. As with all genuine dilemmas, there is no easy answer, but you can have a very valuable discussion about what they think the most likely outcome might be.

Linking to writing

This unit is full of opportunities to develop the 'creating and shaping texts' objectives from the *Primary Framework for literacy*. You will need to do some very structured teaching of this during your writing lessons, but the drama will offer a very rich context for the children to put their developing skills into practice.

Guidance on assessment

Any assessment of this work will be related back to the Key learning for drama, which stated that by the end of this unit the children will have:

- taken roles as experts in marketing and public relations and responded to their teacher in role – *do they take these on convincingly, using appropriate language and behaviour?*
- worked in their expert roles to prepare and present a case – *do they use their chosen media to present a clear case for re-opening the railway?*
- created a still–move–still structure to explore reactions in the local community – *are these clear and well controlled? Do they understand the difference between the case they presented as 'experts' and the feelings in the local area?*
- worked in a second role as members of the local community – *do they adapt to this second role and sustain it through the meeting?*
- reflected on a number of issues and possibilities and physically represented some of the tensions between them – *how much do their responses show that they have engaged with and understood the issues?*

Adapting this unit

Although we have chosen a local railway line as a context, the approaches outlined in this unit could be adapted for a range of environmental issues. It is very similar in structure to the example of the reservoir drama given in *Beginning Drama 4–11* (Winston and Tandy, 3rd edition, 2008). It is also very adaptable in terms of age range, but you would probably expect older children to produce a more coherent and complex case for re-opening the railway, and show a deeper understanding of the complexity of the issues.

4F | Space

Where this unit fits in

In this unit, children will create their own radio programme about space. An interviewer will meet a group of astronauts during their last hours before lift-off, describe the launch from the ground and then hand over to them in the shuttle. They will then describe how it feels to be inside the shuttle during launch.

The recording equipment needed for this project does not need to be sophisticated; a simple tape-recorder or Dictaphone would do the job. What the children will really enjoy is finding ways to make their recordings sound as authentic as possible. Not only will they plan the dialogue carefully but they will also consider the types of background sounds necessary to depict where the recording is supposed to be taking place.

The ideas in this unit are based on a fascinating account of space travel, written by a real 'astronaut blogger' by the name of Leroy Chiao. His vivid descriptions prove an exciting and accessible read. You can access them at http://leroychiao.blogspot.com.

Key learning

Key learning for drama

By the end of this unit, the children will have:

- worked as a group to develop a fictional interview;
- described, in role as astronauts, the appearance of the shuttle, using pictures and words as a guide;
- taken different roles within a group;
- developed a 30-word description of take-off, using film as a stimulus;
- changed sections of a written report to a radio report, presented in the present tense.

Primary Framework for literacy objectives

- Speaking – tell stories effectively and convey detailed information coherently for listeners; respond appropriately to the contributions of others.
- Group discussion and interaction – take different roles in groups and use the language appropriate to them, including the roles of leader, reporter, scribe and mentor.
- Drama – develop scripts based on improvisation; comment constructively on performances, discussing effects and how they are achieved.

Resources

- Recording equipment – exactly what depends on what you have available in school, but remember, the project can still work well with a simple tape-recorder or Dictaphone for each group; and all PCs have a very simple accessory called 'Sound Recorder' which records sound, and more complex programs such as 'Audacity' are freely available.
- A short example of a film showing a shuttle launch (access from the NASA website).

- Picture/diagram of the outside of a space shuttle (labelled).
- Description of a launch written by an astronaut.
- Flip chart and pens.

Steps for teaching and learning

Step 1: A few hours before lift-off . . .

Organise children into groups of four or five. Choose a child in each group to be the interviewer; the other children will take the roles of astronauts.

To begin with, each group will need to think of some questions that would be suitable to ask an astronaut in the last few hours before the flight, and these questions could provide a picture of what the astronauts have felt and experienced up to that moment. Their questions might include:

- 'What preparations have you needed to make before lift-off?'
- 'How much sleep were you able to get last night?'
- 'What are you looking forward to most?'
- 'What sort of food will you be eating in space?'
- 'What sort of clothes will you be wearing?'
- 'When you are in space, how will you go to the toilet?'

Obviously, the children will need to research the questions they have chosen carefully, and because they will want to sound like real astronauts, their research will have a clear focus.

The first thing that Leroy Chiao describes in his blog is the last breakfast he eats before leaving Earth and heading into space. The breakfast table is a great place for children to start their radio programme. Before the interviewer asks the questions the group has prepared, they might begin with a description of each breakfast that the astronauts have chosen as their last meal before they leave Earth.

They can add the sounds of clattering plates, knives and forks throughout the scene to add to the authenticity of the interview.

Before the children record the clip, they will need to practise who will respond to the questions and how. It will not sound very natural if they answer all the questions one by one. Even when one person answers, everyone must respond in some way. For example, if someone makes a comment that everyone agrees with, some 'hmms' and 'yeahs' in the background will make the recording sound live and real. The great thing about sound recording is that children can get immediate feedback on how they sound and re-record as necessary.

Step 2: The astronauts approach the shuttle

Split the description of the exterior of the space craft between two of the astronauts. The other members of the group can act as directors and recording technicians at this stage. The children should think of one simple but open-ended question for the interviewer to ask, for example: 'So we're walking towards the craft now, it's an amazing sight. Can you describe for our listeners exactly what you can see in front of you?'

The two astronauts should describe their answer in as much detail as possible. To help them, provide a detailed, labelled picture of the exterior of a space shuttle, so that they can use the correct technical language and describe it clearly.

Make sure the children do not expect to make a recording of this the first time. It will need careful practice. Other members of the group should be listening with a very critical ear to pick up when there is too much hesitation or too many empty spaces. It is very likely that, as the ideas develop, the children will want to jot down a few simple notes, so reassure them that this is typical of the sort of preparation radio presenters have to do.

Once the description is ready to be recorded, remind children to think about authenticity. It is unlikely that the interviewer will just listen. They are far more likely to add interjections such as 'Really?' or 'That's amazing'.

The other thing for the children to consider is how they are going to make the recording sound as though they are standing outdoors. One option is that the recording actually takes place outdoors, another is that outdoor sounds are added as another layer onto the recording. The second approach sounds more professional, but clearly depends on the equipment you have available, but the first can be very creative and plenty of fun.

Step 3: Take-off

Now it is the job of the interviewer to describe what take-off looks like from the ground, but the whole group will need to develop their ideas together, and be ready to act as members of a 'crowd'.

The best way to develop ideas is to watch a short film clip (no longer than two minutes) of a shuttle taking off. There are many examples on the Internet, particularly the excellent NASA website, and if you have Digital Blue movie creators in school, they have a stock clip of a take-off. Show the clip to the whole class, but make sure they sit in their groups so they can pool ideas ready for their radio programme. Give each group one sheet of flip-chart paper divided into four sections, and some marker pens.

When the children watch the clip for the first time, ask them to think hard about how it makes them feel as they watch the shuttle leave the ground – are they exhilarated? Jealous? Awe-struck? Then allow them one minute to write down as many responses as they can in the first section of the paper.

Show the clip again. This time, ask the children to look carefully at all the different things that they can see happening to the craft itself. After they have seen it, give them a minute to discuss and write down everything they can remember, in order.

The third time the children watch the clip, ask them to concentrate on the sounds they can hear. Again, give them a minute to record their responses. Finally, ask the children to write down any other interesting things they would like to add in section four. These could include questions such as, 'I wonder how it must feel to be inside the shuttle at this moment?'

Once the children have collected all their ideas, ask them to write an exciting description of lift-off in no more than 30 words, which must include at least one word or phrase from each section of the paper. You may decide to allow them to work in pairs or threes at this point so each child is more actively engaged in the process.

The group must then decide on their final 30-word description, and prepare to record the interviewer reading it out. Although it will be scripted, it is important it sounds spontaneous and fresh – real skills for the writer and broadcaster. One way of achieving this is to actually have the film playing in the background as the children make the recording, so it actually sounds like the interviewer is standing near to where a shuttle is taking off. The other children in the group should think about the sort of crowd noises that might be heard in the background. The odd 'Look at that!', or 'Wow!' in the distance (and it does need to sound distant) can work very effectively.

Step 4: How the launch feels inside the shuttle

Now the interviewer will do the sound recording as the astronauts describe what a launch feels like from the inside of the shuttle. Give out four parts of a description of a launch, written by a real astronaut, which can be easily accessed from Leroy Chiao's blog (http://leroychiao.blogspot.com/2009/05/life-in-space-beginning-space-shuttle.html). He describes the experience in extraordinary detail, from the energy and power of the lift-off to the experience of weightlessness. There is plenty of wonderful description on the website and obviously you will want to adapt the phrases and differentiate them depending on the ability of the children. The first thing the children need to do is to change each phrase so it sounds like it is happening now, for example:

> Two minutes have passed and the solid rocket boosters are tailing off, they've consumed the last bits of fuel!

Remind children that the phrases they have read have been written by astronauts who have had time to think about them. An astronaut talking 'live' through lift-off might have a particular mix of measured, professional calm and real excitement – a real challenge for even your most able children to think about. Each astronaut should have their own phrase to say. The child taking the role of interviewer, who will not be speaking in this part, should move from one 'astronaut' to another, asking them to read out their adapted phrases as they go along, offering any further advice or suggestions.

Next, they must think of the delivery. It would help to show the children a clip of something like a 'Blue Peter Challenge' to remind them of how it might feel to be involved in an extreme pursuit, whilst having to speak at the same time. It will also be very useful if you can give them examples of radio broadcasts that do the same – the BBC website has plenty of examples through their 'Listen again' facility.

To make the broadcast more authentic, the children might want to sit in similar positions to those of the astronauts. For example, all the astronauts might choose to sit in very close proximity to each other. Gym mats could be spread out in the hall so that, if necessary, the children can sit or lie at an angle.

The 'interviewer' is acting as director in this scene, so they need to decide which order the phrases will be placed in. Once they are happy with the order and the style of delivery, they can make their recording.

Step 5: Rounding off the programme

The children may want to make this sound as if it is in the first episode in a series of radio programmes about space, so they should think hard about how it should end. As a final scene, the interviewer could communicate, as if via satellite, with the astronauts in space. After all the excitement of the launch, it is easy to forget that the real work starts once the astronauts are in space.

The children will really enjoy piecing together their ideas. Because they will be so keen to make their programme sound as realistic as possible, they will try hard to find out all the right facts, and those children in the class who are already extremely knowledgeable about space will be in their element. Their research may lead them to understand all sorts of purposes of space travel and research, which touch on all sorts of issues – for example about the environment – which you might pursue through further drama, speaking and listening, reading and writing.

Guidance for assessment

Any assessment of this work will be related back to the Key learning for drama, which stated that by the end of this unit, the children will have:

- worked as a group to develop a fictional interview – *does every child in the group have a role? Is everyone on task? Do the questions reflect the style of a radio report?*
- in role as astronauts, described the appearance of the shuttle, using pictures and words as a guide – *do the children use appropriate technical language in their description? How smooth and believable is the eventual delivery?*
- taken different roles within a group – *is this done successfully?*
- developed a 30-word description of take-off, using film as a stimulus – *how effective are their word choices? How spontaneous does the account sound when it is recorded?*
- changed sections of a written report to a radio report, presented in the present – *to what extent does the style and order of the language reflect that of a real radio report?*

Adapting this unit

This unit is based on space travel fact, rather than science fiction. Children across the 7–11 age range are often fascinated by the realities of space travel, and this unit could readily be adapted for them. If you want to extend it further, you might use the same approach for describing new and undiscovered worlds.

4P | *The Comedy of Errors*

This unit is based on *The Comedy of Errors*, by William Shakespeare.

Where this unit fits in

This comedy plays with the themes of twins and mistaken identity. A merchant of Syracuse, Egeon, has been condemned to death because he has passed from his home city into the rival city of Ephesus. When faced with execution, he tells the Duke the sad story of how his family were separated in a shipwreck. Egeon himself was left with the eldest of his twin sons while his wife (he assumed) took care of the younger. Egeon had bought another pair of twin babies from a poor family who would grow to be manservants to his sons. These too were also split, one staying with Egeon, the other (so he thought) with his wife and younger son.

Now 18, the eldest son, Antipholus of Syracuse, and his manservant have decided to seek their missing brothers. Egeon has decided to follow them which is why he has arrived in Ephesus. The fun really begins when the two sets of twins end up in the same city, having no idea that their identical brothers are meeting and confusing the same people.

The plot itself can be very complicated in places and the script difficult to follow for Year 4. We suggest splitting the story up into three parts.

In Scene 1, Egeon tells his story, using language from the script, accompanied by special torch lighting effects. The second scene will open without any language at all; the confusion and actions will be developed through mime. In the final part of the second scene, the children will perform a sound poem, made up of angry lines from confused citizens. The last scene will involve just the last few lines from the play, which tie all the ends together. If the children are not performing lines from the script, they will be involved in sound effects created by the crowd.

Although you will need to choose children to play the main characters in the play (Egeon, the two sets of twins, the Abbess, Adriana and Antonio) there are no small parts. It is as much fun to be part of the crowd as it is to be a character written into the script.

Key learning

Key learning for drama

By the end of this unit the children will have:

- created a shipwreck scene through improvisation, using lighting effects;
- taken part in a mimed crowd scene;
- performed a performance poem created through improvisation;
- followed and learnt their part in a script and rehearsed and performed it.

Primary Framework for literacy objectives

- Speaking – tell stories effectively and convey detailed information coherently for listeners.
- Drama – create roles showing how behaviour can be interpreted from different viewpoints; develop scripts based on improvisation; comment constructively on plays and performances, discussing effects and how they are achieved.

Resources

- Torches – enough for every child. We suggest asking the children to bring them in from home.
- Copies of Act I Scene 1 and Act V Scene 1 (you will need to prepare this yourself, making decisions about the cuts you want to make and the lines you want to retain).
- A space where children can rehearse (preferably the same as their performance space).

Steps for teaching and learning

Step 1: The storm in improvisation

Egeon's long speeches in Act I Scene 1 paint a vivid picture of the shipwreck, when his family were separated. Every child in the play can help to bring the shipwreck to life by creating simple yet clever lighting effects, using torches.

Children will need time to practise the effects that their torches can create. Begin by playing 'torch-bearers'. Organise children into groups of four or five and then darken the room. Call out a mixture of interesting phrases, and lines from the play which children will represent with still or moving torch light. After you have called out each line, give the children up to four minutes to discuss, decide on, then rehearse an idea. Remind them that they should start and finish together. Choose a director in each group to guide the final decision: if each child has a number, you can call out a different one each time so the job is shared around. The phrases might include:

- 'Spotlight';
- 'Obscured light';
- 'Confusion';
- 'Sun gazing upon the earth';
- 'floating straight';

- 'seas waxed calm';
- 'we were encountered by a mighty rock!'

Step 2: How the storm might be created

It is not necessary to include every line of Egeon's speech. Just piece together the lines that you think are important to the story but, as much as possible, use Shakespeare's language. Children at this age can enjoy the sounds and rhythms as they play with it, without getting too hung up on its exact meaning. We offer some suggestions for how the lighting effects might be choreographed with language, but this will grow out of your children's play and experimentation.

Begin with the children sitting in a circle with torches facing downwards. The light in the room should be as low as possible. Egeon should be sitting in the centre of the circle, the only person without a torch. Decide whether the child you have chosen to play Egeon performs all the lines or whether the torch-bearers join in with some of the lines to tell the story.

We suggest that the Duke himself does not need to be on stage at all; an offstage voice from someone who cannot be seen, perhaps speaking into a microphone, is all that is needed to suggest a God-like voice of judgement.

> DUKE: If any Syracusian born
> Come to the bay of Ephesus – he dies,
> *(We would suggest a cut to . . .)*
> Unless a thousand marks be levied
> To quit the penalty and ransom him.
> Thy substance, valued at the highest rate,
> Cannot amount unto a hundred marks,
> Therefore by law thou art condemned to die

The children will need certain cues for their lighting effects. At the start, the torches might be positioned at floor-level pointing towards

the centre and the word 'die' might be the cue for other stage lights
to be turned off and all the torches to be switched on.

> EGEON: In Syracusa was I born, and wed
> And married, lived in joy, our wealth increased

When Egeon says the word 'born' the torches might point towards his
face, creating a spotlight, or you may decide to pick out one
particularly strong torch to shine towards him and have the other
torches pointing downwards.

There are several key moments that show important parts of the
shipwreck. The lines that describe the likeness between the boys are
important:

> the one so like the other
> As could not be distinguished but by names.

At this point, you might have two pairs of children stepping into
opposite ends of the circle; Antipholus and Dromio of Syracuse at
one end and Antipholus and Dromio of Ephesus at the other. For
your performance, each set of twins should be wearing identical
clothing. You might use half-masks, or even identical pairs of silly
glasses that cover the face without interfering with speech. When
Egeon says the word 'one', they might shine their torch underneath
their own faces, and on the word 'other' they might angle the
torchlight onto the face of their 'twin'.

The description of the storm scene is where the effects can become
really exciting. When Egeon says:

> Alas! Too soon
> We came aboard.

You may want the children to move out of the circle shape and into a
shape that represents a ship's stern. All the torches can then be

pointed forward into the audience, then turned off at the same time.
Egeon describes how the storm builds:

> For what obscured light the heavens did grant
> Did but convey unto our fearful minds
> A doubtful warrant of immediate death,

At this point, the light from the torches might dance around, pointed
towards the ceiling (as if referring to 'the heavens'). The last line
would work particularly well if it was said by everyone, the word
'death' acting as a cue for a particularly dramatic effect, such as the
children suddenly holding the torches underneath their chins so the
light shining upwards gives them a ghostly appearance.

> The children thus disposed, my wife and I,
> Fixing our eyes on whom our care was fixed,
> Fastened ourselves at either end the mast,

When Egeon describes how he and his wife fastened themselves and
their children to the mast, Egeon, the two sets of twins and a child
you have chosen to play Egeon's wife step into the centre. A smaller
group of torch-bearers might surround them, crouching close to the
ground, pointing their torches upwards so that their light joins
together above the heads of Egeon's family. This would represent the
mast.

Just before the point when Egeon mentions the other ships in the
distance who have come to save them ...

> Two ships from far, making amain to us,
> Of Corinth that, of Epidaurus this.

... have some of your torch-bearers move to the back of the audience,
turning on the torches and sweeping them from side to side, pointing
to the front of the stage to show that ships are coming closer.

The 'mighty rock' can be created simply and effectively with half of the group moving into the centre, crouched down with their heads and arms tucked in, turning the ground into a curvy surface. The torches can then skim the surface of the 'rocks'.

After Egeon describes the fateful split from his wife and that of the two sets of brothers, he then goes on to explain that he is searching for the son that he has looked after until the age of 18. At this point, Antipholus of Syracuse and his manservant Dromio of Syracuse should step forward and all the torches should be directed onto them.

Then, to signify their journey forward, all the torch-bearers could move out of their circle and form two parallel lines like sides of a road, shining their torches ahead. Antipholus and Dromio can then walk down this 'road' as the Duke speaks his last words in this scene to Egeon:

> DUKE: Try all the friends thou hast in Ephesus
> Beg thou or borrow to make up the sum,
> And live. If no, then thou art doomed to die.
> *Egeon is accompanied off stage by a jailer.*

Step 3: Mistaken identity – a mime

Following the last scene, the children walk off stage, re-entering, without torches, as characters in the crowd of the busy centre of Ephesus. Echoing the two halves of the ship, the children should be grouped into two halves at either end of the stage. To begin with, they move into position and freeze.

The next part of the story is told through mime. The Syracuse twins start on one half, and the Ephesus twins on the other. Light and cheerful background music will help to create the atmosphere: as soon as it starts, the crowd should start interacting, talking to each other, buying, selling and gossiping. The two sets of twins start to cross from one side of the stage to the other, narrowly missing each other, and frequently getting mixed up as master and servant. Choose some of the events that happen in the play to show to the audience. For example, Dromio is unfairly beaten for losing money he was never given, Antonio accuses Antipholus of Ephesus of stealing a chain that has never passed into his hands, and Antipholus of Syracuse is seduced by a wife he didn't realise he had. Different parts of the mime could be choreographed to fit in with the music if it has been chosen carefully. The end of the miming sequence needs to show Antipholus and Dromio of Syracuse running into the Abbey for safety – this is easy to suggest on stage by a child wearing a nun's veil appearing from the back of the stage and simply standing in front of them.

Step 4: The angry crowd

Following the mime, the scene should reach a crescendo, where there is a terrible cacophony in the crowd and a build up of anger and confusion. This can take the form of a rhythmic performance poem which the class can develop using their own ideas. Ask the children to think of a range of other unfortunate scenarios that might occur when two people who share exactly the same appearance stumble into the same place by accident. Give them time to discuss ideas in pairs and, if you feel it is appropriate, ask them to write them down. The children will then need to choose one of their ideas and turn it into a simple phrase that has a rhythm so that it can be easily repeated over a beat. For example:

I asked him for my money but he says he owes me nothing.

or

I thought he was my friend but now he says he's never met me.

To create this in the performance, stop the music and have the characters standing still for a moment. Have one child (who might be dressed like a clock-maker) beat time with a wood block. They should walk in and out of the crowd and as they pass each child, one at a time they will join in the rhythm by walking around the stage and repeating their own phrase. Eventually every child on the stage will be part of the sound poem. At this point, Egeon re-enters the stage, pushed roughly by a guard. His time has run out, and he is about to face death.

Step 5: Egeon's family reunited

We suggest that to tell the final part of the story, the children perform the play from Act V Scene 1, line 332 onwards. As in the first scene, pick the lines that you think will work best in telling the story. This part of the script is quite accessible and very funny. All the action in this scene requires interaction from the crowd, and there is a lot of quick interplay between the characters. The noisy atmosphere that has been created in the last scene will provide an opportunity for the Abbess to make an impressive entrance by dramatically silencing the din:

ABBESS: Most mighty Duke, behold a man much wronged.

The crowd fall silent, then move to the back of the stage and form a semicircle facing the front. This echoes the circle they created at the beginning. Just as in the first scene, the cast are going to work together to produce an effect, except this time they are going to create sounds.

Improvise, using the same structure as the torch-bearer game. Again, ask the children to move into groups, and call out a selection of phrases that they will respond to with an expression such as:

- shock;
- confusion;
- disbelief;
- joy;
- amusement.

As you did before, allow the groups a few minutes to discuss and rehearse their ideas. Pick out some examples that worked well, then read through the script with the children, asking them at which points in the script it would be appropriate to use these reactions. For example, the exchange between Adriana and Antipholus of Syracuse and Antipholus of Ephesus:

> ADRIANA: Are you not my husband?
> ANTIPHOLUS OF EPHESUS: No, I say nay to that.

This might be greeted by a great guffaw from the crowd with a hand to the mouth, or a questioning 'Nay?' with a hand on the hip. It is quite appropriate for this scene to have a slapstick quality. However, do explain that some expressions will work well in unison, whereas others should not all occur at the same moment. Sometimes the crowd needs to sound more natural – more like a rabble than a choir – and each character should have their own gesture for each expression. This will take a lot of rehearsal, but it will really add to the impact of the final scene.

In Shakespeare's original script, the play ends with all the characters offstage except for the two Dromios. We would suggest that you turn the lights off, and a small group of children shine their torches on them as they speak their last lines:

> DROMIO OF EPHESUS: We came into the world brother and brother,
> And now let's go hand in hand, not one before another.

Guidance on assessment

Any assessment of this work will be related back to the Key learning for drama, which stated that by the end of this unit the children will have:

- created a shipwreck scene through improvisation, using lighting effects – *how well do the children work as part of an ensemble? Do they move effectively in unison?*
- taken part in a mimed crowd scene – *can the children express themselves effectively by acting through their bodies?*
- performed a performance poem created through improvisation – *how confidently do the children combine the line with the rhythm? Are they able to stay in role?*
- followed and learnt their part in a script and rehearsed and performed it – *does their performance of Shakespeare's words show an understanding of the story, through expression and intonation?*

Adapting this unit

Although this work is challenging for Year 4, its reliance on sound, light and movement will make a complex play accessible to them. The approach would work well with older children and could certainly be adapted to other plays.

5L | *The Listeners*

This unit is based on *The Listeners*, by Walter de la Mare.

Where this unit fits in

This mysterious poem is filled with intriguing unanswered questions. An unnamed traveller knocks upon the door of a mysterious house, asking 'is there anybody there?' When there is no response he 'smotes upon the door' a second time, repeating his question. Although his persistence is met with nothing but silence, the reader knows that 'the listeners' have heard everything, and not until the traveller has ridden away on his horse does their silence 'surge softly backward'. What makes this poem irresistible is that we don't know who or what the listeners are. We know them only as a 'host of phantom listeners'. But are they silent because they are afraid? Or is it that they want to speak but physically they cannot? Are they literal phantoms, supernatural beings who have crossed from life to death, and if so, what do they know of the traveller's fate? Could they be animals or birds, or the inanimate contents of the empty house?

The drama work in this unit will provide the inspiration for children to produce a piece of descriptive writing from the point of view of 'The Observer' – an innocent onlooker who has written a diary entry about the strange things they have witnessed.

This poem provides exciting opportunities for historical investigation. How were messages sent more than 100 years ago? What were the options for conveying the message? How could you deliver a message without speaking at the time *The Listeners* was written? When was the first time that you didn't have to deliver a message in person? This could be compared with the ways messages are sent today.

Key learning

Key learning for drama

By the end of this unit, the children will have:

- explored and recited lines from a text in a variety of ways;
- collaborated in groups to create a title and a still image, based on evidence;
- moved from group to whole-class work, sequencing chosen events;
- used text and images to help them to create a spoken landscape;
- captured their experiences in writing.

Primary Framework for literacy objectives

- Speaking – tell a story using notes designed to cue techniques, such as repetition, recap and humour.
- Group discussion and interaction – plan and manage a group task over time using different levels of planning; understand different ways to take the lead and support others in groups.
- Drama – reflect on how working in role helps to explore complex issues; improvise using a range of drama strategies and conventions to explore themes.
- Understanding and interpreting texts: infer writers' perspectives from what is written and from what is implied; explore how writers use language for dramatic effects.

Resources

- Copies of the poem – one per child.
- A supply of different individual lines from the poem, large and clear.
- Pictures of possible settings for the poem – one per group of three.
- An example of a similar poetry or prose (for extension work) such as *The Highwayman*, by Alfred Noyes.

Steps for teaching and learning

Step 1: Introducing the poem

Sit the whole class in a circle. Choose four children (who are sitting at intervals in the circle) to come out to you and receive a message which they must pass around the circle no louder than a whisper. The rest of the class should have no idea what the messages are. They will be four key lines from the poem:

- Is there anybody there?
- tap on the moonlit door
- tell them that I came and no-one answered
- 'I kept my word,' he said.

The children return to their places in the circle, two of them passing the messages clockwise and the other two anticlockwise: the messages will cross in the middle.

When you feel the messages have been sent around far enough, ask the children to speak out the lines they think they have heard. Even though they have only been provided with four lines, they can begin to piece together some good ideas about the poem. Asking questions like these can deepen thinking:

- Why might messages like this need to be passed in this way?
- Did everyone hear the same things?

- If people misheard the messages, how did this change the meaning or the emphasis?
- What might be the consequence of misunderstanding a message?
- Who might be delivering a message like this?
- Who is 'he'?
- Who are 'they'?
- Do you think the messenger got the response they expected?

Reveal that the four lines are from a poem. Ask the children to work in groups of four or five and explain that this poem has been published many times as a book, usually with a very striking picture on the cover. Based on the four lines you have shared and the ideas generated in discussion, ask the children to think of a possible title for the poem and to create a still image to show what the book cover might look like. When the children have had time to explore, ask each group to find their own space. When prompted, they should call out the title of the poem and form the still image.

Encourage children to consider what these 'book covers' can tell us about the poem. How can they describe the body language? Examples could be 'stiff fingers', 'eyes frozen', 'whispering lips'. When used in writing, such vivid details grip the reader; it is easy for them to imagine the physical reactions in their own bodies and the emotions that cause them. By this point, children will be eager to read the whole poem. After holding it back for just long enough, this is the point to share it.

Step 2: Reading and understanding the poem

Read and discuss the poem with the children. Make sure that they are familiar with the events. Next, use tableaux as a device to help them sequence events and to explore the concepts imaginatively. Ask children to work in groups of four or five. Explain that they are going to be 'the listeners' at three different points in the poem. They must create a still image for each line:

1   'Is there anybody there?'
2   'Tell them I came and no-one answered, that I kept my word ... '
3   And how the silence surged softly backward when the plunging hooves were gone.

When the children have practised, arrange the groups in a circle, ready to get into position. Darken the room and stand in the centre of the circle, holding a strong torch. Explain that when you call out one of the three lines and shine the torch on a specific group, they, and they alone, should change to the next tableau, but in absolute silence. But if you point the torch at the ceiling and say the line, all the groups must form their chosen tableaux for that line at the same time. As they wait for the torch to shine upon them or at the ceiling, they should stay in their present position with as little movement as possible. The dramatic shadows cast on the walls around the room heighten the mysterious atmosphere.

Step 3: Exploring and capturing ideas for writing

If the children are to create a piece of descriptive writing from the point of view of 'the observer', they will need to include three main elements: what they notice about the traveller and how he moves; the sounds that can be heard; and visual details about the forest and the house. The following activity encourages children to explore the text and use it to develop language for a spoken landscape.

Ask the children to move into groups of three. They are now going to gather as many ideas as they can about the scene in the poem by creating the most haunting setting that they can, using movement and spoken words.

Provide the children with the poem, pictures of a suitable scene (such as an old haunted house or a spooky forest) and, if possible, play an atmospheric soundtrack or sound effects in the background. For children who need further challenge, you may also provide them with a verse from a similar poem (such as *The Highwayman*, by Alfred Noyes) or prose that describes a similar setting. Give the children some highlighter pens and encourage them to highlight all the atmospheric detail they can pick out, both in the text and in the picture. When the children highlight the picture, encourage them to annotate the details, so they have lines that they will be able to use later on. Give the children about five minutes to notice as much as they can.

Step 4: Speaking the setting

The children now need to have a number: one, two or three. Number ones are going to be the traveller, numbers two and three are going to walk one step behind, each with a hand on the traveller's shoulder. Numbers two and three will be voices in the traveller's head, describing what he sees in front of him. The hands on the shoulders will push the traveller forward. Sometimes they might lead the traveller to crawl on the floor or take some steps back. This works particularly well if the traveller has their eyes closed, but this is optional. This activity creates an imaginary landscape for the person in front; those following can watch them react to the atmosphere they create. As there is more than one child providing the description, they will support each other's ideas. For example:

> Look at the ground. It is all bumpy with fern. Stop! A centipede has just scuttled over your shoe. It makes you shudder. You are getting nearer and nearer to the crumbling house. The door is lit with moonlight, but it is the only light in the house.

Swap the trios around so that all the children have the opportunity to describe the setting and to take the part of the traveller. There are several ways of adapting and extending this activity. For example, one of the two voices can be positive, the other negative, for example:

> VOICE A: There is someone watching in the trees, they are whispering – you must not go on.
> VOICE B: Stay strong, the whispering is only the sound of the breeze in the leaves.

77

Another way of using this idea is that one of the 'voices' provides description whilst the other creates sound effects or actions. So, for example, 'Stop! A centipede has scuttled over your foot'! might be accompanied by either a scuttling sound in the ear of the traveller or gentle tapping on the traveller's shoe.

Step 5: Writing the words of a silent observer

Provide the children with a generous supply of scrap paper (about A5 size) and some marker pens. Explain that they are going to be the listeners, creating everything that they have witnessed but, as in the poem, they must be completely silent, so they must use written words and phrases. These should be written on the paper (one word or phrase per piece of paper – large and clear enough for others to read) and spread out across the floor like a carpet. This should include words describing how the traveller reacted (for example, 'He shuddered as a centipede scuttled over his foot'), small details about the house and the forest (for example, 'Behind him the trunks and branches of ancient trees winced in the bitter night'), and sounds (for example, 'Twigs creaked and snapped underfoot').

By exploring the text through drama, children will have found unique ways to express what they have acted and felt. The words spread across the floor will provide you with a powerful resource from which you can draw endless ideas for writing.

Before asking children to produce their diary entry, written as the observer, it is important that the teacher models the writing. Naturally, you will remind them of the processes, structures and conventions they have been learning about in other literacy lessons. But, as well as this, you can take ideas directly from their word carpet. This way, they will be learning how to thread together the imaginative ideas that they as a whole class have shared. And they will see how reading and writing can be enriched through the power of experience.

Guidance on assessment

Any assessment of this work will be related back to the Key learning for drama, which stated that by the end of this unit the children will have:

* explored and recited lines from a text in a variety of ways – *are the children able to pick up on the rhythm in the lines? Do they transfer the language to their own descriptions, both verbal and written?*
* collaborated in a group to create a title and a still image, based on evidence – *how well do the children use the evidence they have to make meaningful suggestions? How well do they participate in making decisions as part of a team?*
* moved from group to whole-class work, sequencing chosen events – *how measured and disciplined are the children as a group and/or individuals when moving in a large space with a large group?*
* used text and images to help them to create a spoken landscape – *how well do they suspend the illusion for the traveller through movement, sound and words?*
* captured their experiences in writing – *have the children used their experiences in drama to describe the sensations the traveller might have experienced?*

Adapting this unit

All the activities in this unit – the still images, word carpet and spoken landscape – can be adapted for other lessons. The work in this unit has a strong focus on character and setting, so work on mystery and adventure stories, myths, legends and traditional tales could be explored using these approaches.

5C Howard Carter and Tutankhamen

This unit is based on the study of the Ancient Egyptians from the history curriculum, focusing on Howard Carter and the discovery of the tomb of Tutankhamen.

Where this unit fits in

The discovery of the tomb of Tutankhamen was one of the most important events in twentieth-century archaeology. It was particularly significant because the tomb and its contents had been undisturbed from the time of the young Pharaoh's burial. It caused a great deal of media excitement at the time and the story still has enormous appeal. Children at this age will enjoy not only the story of the discovery, but also the stories about the 'curse', as well as some of the details about mummification and burial. It can also lead them into some very deep thinking about the rights and wrongs of archaeology and the extent to which people should continue to have respect for ancient civilisations and their beliefs.

This unit derives directly from the world history study in the National Curriculum for history. Ancient Egypt is only one of the options for a past society to study, but it is one of the most frequently chosen by schools, not least because of the abundance of resources available. Some schools choose to combine their history work with a geographical study which looks at a locality in Egypt today.

As well as the very strong links with art and music through this unit, it also offers plenty of opportunities for developing writing. With its focus on beliefs about death and the afterlife, and issues of cultural understanding, it also connects strongly with the Religious Education curriculum and Personal, Social and Health Education.

The drama work outlined in this unit is likely to work best if it takes place towards the end of the history unit so that children can use their knowledge of Ancient Egypt to inform their work.

Key learning

Key learning for drama

By the end of this unit, the children will have:

- created tableaux and spoken 'headlines' to represent how the story of the discovery of the tomb and the events surrounding Lord Carnarvon's death were reported in the newspapers at the time;
- explored through mime the idea of precious gifts and artefacts and how people handle them;
- collaborated to create and perform a dramatised ritual burial of the Pharaoh;
- responded to teacher in role while remaining in role themselves.

Primary Framework for literacy objectives

- Speaking – present a spoken argument, sequencing points logically, defending views with evidence and making use of persuasive language.
- Listening – analyse the use of persuasive language.
- Drama – reflect on how working in role helps to explore complex issues; use and recognise the impact of theatrical effects in drama.

Resources

- Access to a good-sized, clear space, probably the hall. It will be very helpful if this space can be blacked out, or at least darkened as much as possible.
- A range of musical instruments and a reasonably powerful torch.

Steps for teaching and learning

Step 1: Stories of the curse and the death of Lord Carnarvon

Before you begin this work, it will be helpful if children know a little of the story of the discovery of Tutankhamen's tomb, the roles of Howard Carter and Lord Carnarvon, and the events surrounding Carnarvon's death. Talk to them about how stories of 'the curse' might have arisen, and ask them to think about how Carnarvon's death might have been reported in the newspapers of the day.

In groups, ask the children to create still images (tableaux) to show pictures that might have appeared on the front pages of the papers. Then ask them to create a 'headline' to accompany their picture. Rather than review the pictures individually, ask all the groups to make them simultaneously, then tell them that as you move among them you want to hear the headline that accompanies each. The headline may be spoken by an individual, by different children taking a word or a few words each, or by the whole group speaking it in unison. You can then move among the images, pausing by each group as they speak out their headline. You can also experiment with speaking the headlines all at once by asking the groups to repeat them over and over.

At the end of this activity, explain to the children that you are going to explore the story further to see how legends of the curse might have arisen and, if there ever was such a thing, how and why it might have been put on the Pharaoh's tomb in the first place.

82

Step 2: Imagining treasures

Discuss what the children know about the kinds of treasures that were found in the tomb, listing as many as you can on a large sheet of paper. The children then work in pairs, standing about 10 feet apart. They take it in turns to imagine one of the treasures and mime carrying it to their partner. As they mime placing it at their partner's feet (or perhaps around their neck, or shoulders) they say what it is, using as rich and descriptive language as possible; for example, 'A wooden chest, coated in plaster and finely painted with scenes of the mighty Pharaoh's life.' When you have allowed the children time to have three or four turns each, get them to record as much of the language as they can before moving on to the next activity.

Next, the pairs combine to make groups of four. They share all the ideas they developed in the paired activity to agree one treasure, or set of treasures, that they can all carry/move and present between them. A group might, for example, decide on a war chariot. The four of them will mime wheeling this in and then – if they have done their research – mime removing the wheels so that the chariot's weight does not distort them. They decide together on the words they will use to describe the chariot which may be spoken by one child, the whole group together, or any other way they choose.

These ideas can be reviewed by seating the whole class in a circle and asking each group in turn to mime bringing their treasures to the middle and describing them for the rest of the group.

Step 3: Creating the ritual of the Pharaoh's burial

In this section of the work, it is important for children to understand that they are not going to re-create the exact ritual that would have accompanied the Pharaoh's burial. Rather they are going to make a ritual using their own ideas to help them imagine why the burial was so important to the people of the time.

Find a way of representing the sarcophagus and place it at one end of the room. This could be as simple as a table or a PE bench with a cloth over it, but it may be something much more elaborate that the children have made in their other work on Ancient Egypt.

The children are already in groups of four from the previous activity. They now need to practise miming carrying their 'gift' (the treasure they carried in the last activity) and presenting it to the Pharaoh. As they present their gift, they announce it with the following form of words:

> Oh Mighty Pharaoh
> We bring you this [whatever the gift]
> That **** in the afterlife!

Each group will need to think how their gift will be important to the Pharaoh in his afterlife. If, for example, they bring a chariot, they may say:

> Oh Mighty Pharaoh
> We bring you this light and swift chariot
> That you might speedily destroy your enemies in the afterlife!

Give each of the groups a number, and then ask the odd-numbered groups to sit along one side of the hall, and the even-numbered groups along the other. The lowest-numbered groups should be at the end of the hall which is furthest from the sarcophagus.

At the end of the hall which is furthest from the sarcophagus, place a small selection of tuned and un-tuned percussion instruments. Group 1 stand and move quietly so that they are just in front of the instruments, ready to mime taking their gift to the Pharaoh. Group 2 stand and then move to sit behind the instruments, ready to play. As Group 1 make their way towards the sarcophagus, Group 2 accompany them with the musical instruments. If you encourage the children who are playing to *watch* the group who are taking their gift, and *listen* to each other, you and they will be surprised and delighted by the music that is created quite spontaneously.

When Group 1 has reached the sarcophagus and presented their gift, they take up the shapes of statues that have been placed around the body of the Pharaoh. Tell them that they will need to hold these shapes for some time, so they need to make sure they have not chosen something too demanding.

Once Group 1 have taken up their shapes as statues, Group 2 take up positions ready to bring in and announce their gift. Group 3 now need to move into position to play the musical instruments. Once Group 2 have presented their gift and taken up their positions, Group 3 can get ready and Group 4 take up their places as musicians. This structure, where each group plays for the group in front of them before taking their own gift to the Pharaoh will work until the last group move in – but by then there will no group left to play for them. The simplest way to deal with this is if you now give them something like a simple drum beat as they move in, present their gifts and take up their statue shapes. Now the whole class will be in place as the statues guarding the Pharaoh's tomb. You may want to practise this two or three times so that the children can do it well enough for it to have a strong sense of ritual and ceremony. Don't be afraid to insist that they get this part right because it will have a significant impact on how the rest of the work develops.

The last element you may want to build into the burial ceremony is the placing of a 'curse' on anyone who enters the tomb hereafter. The children can suggest a form of words which might be spoken by a single voice, perhaps by a group of children, or maybe one voice that is then echoed by the whole class. Once the 'curse' has been placed you can narrate, 'And with those words, the Pharaoh's tomb was sealed forever!', turning the lights out as you do so.

Step 4: The tomb is disturbed

Negotiate with the children that they will perform the ritual once more, that you will narrate how the tomb was sealed up, and then turn the lights out. Then you will narrate, 'The statues had stood guard over the Pharaoh's tomb for over 3,000 years, unmoving and undisturbed. Until one day there came a scratching and a scraping sound. And behind the scratching and scraping sound came a light which burst into the peace of the tomb.' Tell them that when you have said these words you will turn on a torch and shine it over the statues. Get the class to practise keeping as still as possible while the torchlight plays over them.

Now introduce the idea that, although they cannot move, Carter gets the uneasy idea that he can hear the statues speak. If they could speak, what would they have to say? Practise speaking these words in low whispers, and then tell the class that you are going to move into the space with the torch. Once the torch has shone on a statue, it can begin to whisper, repeating the phrase over and over. The nearer you get to the sarcophagus, the louder the whispers become.

Now you are ready to put all the elements together – the burial ceremony, the 'curse', your narration, and the torchlight coming into the tomb and exploring it – to create a powerful whole performance. If you have been insistent that the children perform well, they will be delighted by the power of what they have created.

Step 5: Carter's dream

Tell the class that you are going to create a dream in which Carter sees himself in Tutankhamen's place, surrounded by the statues. In his dream, he can talk to the statues and they can answer. It is, of course, important to stress that there is no record of Carter having any such dream, but that you are using it as a way of exploring what the statues might feel about his intrusion into the tomb.

Taking the role of Carter, lie on the floor in the place of the table/
bench you used to represent the sarcophagus, and get the children to
take up their places as statues. Once you have taken up the position
of the sleeping Carter, the statues begin to whisper (as they did
before), building to a crescendo which causes you to sit up. Now you
can begin talking to the statues, asking them why they disturb your
sleep night after night. From your role as the archaeologist, you can
tell them that you are only collecting the treasures from the tomb so
that people in your time can know how people in their time lived
and what they believed. The children are likely to produce strong
counter-arguments, perhaps telling you that the treasures should
remain undisturbed and that the beliefs of the people who put them
there should be respected. When you feel the conversation has gone
as far as it can, you can return to your sleeping position before
bringing this activity to an end.

Step 6: Where do you stand?

The last activity is likely to provoke some lively discussion about the
rights and wrongs of disturbing the tomb. When the children have
had time to talk and record some of their ideas, tell them that they
are going to make a decision line. One end of the line represents the
view that any remains from the past must be left undisturbed, the
other the view that people may do what they like with archaeological
discoveries. Because you have created a line, there is plenty of room
for views in between these two extremes. In turn, the children make
statements about what they feel as a result of the work they have just
done, then take up a position along the line which corresponds to
that view. Each of these statements can then be recorded on large
sheets of paper and taken back to the classroom to use in further
writing.

Guidance on assessment

Any assessment of this work will be related back to the Key learning for drama, which stated that by the end of this unit the children will have:

- created tableaux and spoken 'headlines' to represent how the story of the discovery of the tomb and the events surrounding Lord Carnarvon's death were reported in the newspapers at the time – *were the tableaux clear and easy for you and the rest of the class to 'read'?*
- explored through mime the idea of precious gifts and artefacts and how people handle them – *you had an opportunity here to see the work of groups and individuals in turn. How rich and varied was the language they used? How well did the mime match the treasure they described?*
- collaborated to create and perform a dramatised ritual burial of the Pharaoh – *this was a complex and demanding piece to put together; how well could they commit to the ceremony and sustain concentration throughout?*
- responded to teacher in role while remaining in role themselves – *how did they react and respond to you during 'Carter's dream'? Were their comments and arguments compatible with their roles as statues/guards?*

Linking to writing

There are plenty of writing opportunities that arise from this work, including:

- diaries – working from Carter's diaries, perhaps writing their own in role as other members of the expedition;
- describing the entry into the tomb – when you have finished performing the ceremony and the torch has shone over the whispering statues, give the children time to record as much of the language used as they can to use in a written description of the entry into the tomb;
- the rights and wrongs of archaeology – all the work in this unit, particularly the last activity, will equip children with plenty of ideas for writing a discussion about what should be done with archaeological finds like this.

Adapting this unit

Making rituals in the way described in this unit can be used with work on other past civilizations, for example the Aztecs. The structure could also be adapted for other work on archaeological finds, for example if you are doing work on the Saxons or the Vikings. Although the unit is written here with a Year 5 class in mind, we have used the ideas and the basic structure right across the 7–11 range.

5F The Invention of Hugo Cabret

This unit is based on *The Invention of Hugo Cabret*, by Brian Selznick, Scholastic, ISBN 978-1-407-10504-8.

Where this unit fits in

A bewitching tale of mystery and adventure unwinds through the black-edged pages of this beautiful novel. At first glance, the book appears to be a hefty read – a challenge for even the most dedicated of young readers. But the book is not exactly as it appears from the cover. When the reader begins the first chapter, they discover there is hardly any text at all but page after page of entrancing black and white sketches. In fact, in the whole book there are 284 pages of original drawings which bring together the worlds of clocks, automata and film. When the text finally does fall onto the page, one is so mesmerised by the action in the cinematic pictures that you simply cannot wait to read what the author has written.

It would be unfair to reveal the whole story – the book does not even have a synopsis on the back cover, but on the front is a round black sticker which simply reads: 'LOOK INSIDE and watch the story unfold.' The book is full of surprises and it is important that you and the class discover its great secrets. A brief outline will give you some context.

Hugo Cabret is a little boy who lives in a room hidden in the walls of a railway station in Paris. Every day he secretly winds up the clocks in the station – it is a vast place and he is meticulous in his work, so the job takes him a long time. He stays hidden in the station because it contains a secret which has become his obsession and his reason for being. The story takes Hugo on great chases through the streets of Paris and introduces him to fascinating characters such as a grumpy old man who runs a toy booth at the train station and an inquisitive little girl who becomes his friend. As the story progresses he learns about mechanisms, art, books and film, and, most of all, he learns how to find the answers to his questions.

Key learning

Key learning for drama

By the end of this unit, the children will have:

- collaborated in pairs to create sound and a movement to represent a clockwork toy;
- moved into a whole-class representation of clockwork;
- collaborated in groups to make decisions about the Great Invention and to produce a short piece of drama;
- collaborated in groups to change movements into still images to be photographed;
- collaborated in groups to move from a still image to a short piece of moving action.

Primary Framework for literacy objectives

- Group discussion and interaction – plan and manage a group task over time using different levels of planning; understand the process of decision-making.
- Drama – use and recognise the impact of theatrical effects in drama; reflect on how working in role helps to explore complex issues.

Resources

- An overhead projector.
- A selection of small mechanical toys and clocks.
- A selection of springs and cogs.
- Digital cameras.
- A laptop/computer and a data projector that can be accessed within the lesson.
- Something that plays mechanical music (like a musical box).
- Cardboard boxes, covered with cloth (enough for one between four).

Steps for teaching and learning

The children are going to use ICT to help them create a presentation that works in the same way as Brian Selznick's book. Using dramatic conventions, the children will create cinematic images. These images will be based on four key themes in the book and, as they are completed, the children will weave a story around them. In short they are creating their own mystery to solve, just like the boy in the story.

Step 1: Mechanisms

Brian Selznick says that he was inspired to write the book after he had read a book about French automata. Give the children a similar starting point – introduce them to some curious mechanical things. Spread the toys across the centre of the room, making sure that there is enough for one between two. The toys you provide can be as simple as those you might find in a Christmas cracker. The most important thing is that they should make a sound.

Organise the children into pairs. Tell them that you are going to wind up a musical jewellery box and as soon as the music begins to play they should walk around the room, moving in and out of the objects noticing as much as they can without touching them.

Then, when the music stops they should find a mechanical toy to stand next to.

Ask the children to play with the toy they have chosen to stand next to. The first thing they must notice is the sound it makes – they need to try to copy this sound with their own voices. The next thing they must do is to create a simple movement for the toy. If you want to encourage the children to be more disciplined, restrict them to using one body part each to make the action – they will need to think creatively for this and their movement will probably be more effective. When the children have had time to explore putting their sound and movements together, ask them to bring the toys back to you (so the centre of the room is clear) and then form a large circle, with partners standing next to each other.

Explain to the children that you are going to be like a large cog moving around the outside of the circle. Every so often, the cog will make contact with a mechanism and something will happen. What you will be doing is walking around the outside of the circle stopping at one pair at a time and tapping them on the back. The chosen pair will move to the centre of the circle and begin their sound and their action. They must keep this going, just like clockwork. When the next pair move to the centre of the circle they should find some way of joining their action to the last group. Eventually this will create a display of human sound and movement, which will work together like a well-oiled machine.

Tell the children that now you are going to act as a film-maker – just like characters in the story. You will want to film the most interesting angles – ask the children for some suggestions and model some ideas. For example, if you lie on the floor and hold the camera upwards, what effect will it have? How can you make the action look taller? Take a shot of no more than 20 seconds, and show it back to the children as instantly as you can. It may be that you cannot show it until the next day, but if you have a data projector and computer to hand, downloading the image and showing it within a few minutes in

93

the same lesson is ideal. Ask them to suggest improvements and then repeat the film. The teacher filming it has two main purposes at this point. One is that you are modelling how to take interesting shots, and the other is that the children can improve their work by watching what they have just done.

Step 2: The Great Invention

Organise children into groups of four or five. Tell the class that the mechanical film you created shows the workings of the inside of an amazing invention. The children have to decide what the invention does and this is where their story will start.

You can talk about the examples of mechanical inventions seen in the story and use many of its pictures to stimulate ideas. You might also refer to other stories or poems that tell tales of strange automata and mechanical things, such as in *The Iron Man*, by Ted Hughes or Phillip Pullman's *Clockwork*.

Once the children have decided on the purpose of the invention, give each group a cardboard box, covered with a cloth. Ask them to imagine that they are a group of inventors who are going to unveil their mechanical object for the first time. They can use a maximum of ten words between them and their action should stop just before the moment when the invention is unveiled. For example: 'We present the incredible clock that can make time stop.'

When they have had time to explore and rehearse this, introduce a further challenge. Now they must think of an interesting 'hook' to go with the introduction of the invention – something that will stop the moment from going exactly to plan. Tell them that they can do anything they like with the box as long as they don't unveil it. For example, they might carry it carefully and set it down, then lift up the cloth at the back and pretend to adjust it (and find that it doesn't work), they can shake it (and pretend something has dropped out) or accidentally knock it over.

Once the children have decided on this, tell them that one of them will act as the camera person. They are going to take photographs rather than film, and are allowed to take no more than three that will display the main pieces of action and tell what is needed of the story. Remind them to think imaginatively about the angles and shots. Show them some of the pictures in the book – some of them blow up the tiniest details such as a startled eye or flailing fingers.

Tell the children that the unveiling of the invention is going to be followed by a chase, which will lead to a cliff-hanger. Their next job is to decide why and how that will happen.

Step 3: Cliff-hangers and chases

There are several cliff-hangers and chases in the story and the reader really feels as though they are caught up in the action. This is because the writer intersperses sections of dramatic writing with pages of cinematic pictures that give the impression of fast movements and hair-raising settings.

Explain to them that they are going to create a chase and a cliff-hanger using four still images only. They can use the camera to help them to suggest height or danger – this will depend on the angles they use.

One of the films mentioned in the book is Harold Lloyd's *Safety Last*, which has the image of him hanging onto the hands of a clock. As the picture is shown in the book, the children will be really excited to see the moving image from the original film. You can use any clip of film that involves a cliff-hanger (a scene from *Raiders of the Lost Ark*, for example), but if you can get hold of the actual film this would be even better. It is easy to access on the Internet, but if there is a problem with showing this to your class, it can be purchased from the British Film Institute website.

Show them a short section of film that shows one character caught in a moment of heightened suspense – the clip should last no more than a minute. Challenge the children to choose one of the movements to copy – everyone in each group sharing the same one. Ask them to try out ways of improving it by making suggestions to each other and trying out new things. Encourage them to notice everything they can about its physicality. How can you show fear in your eyes? How can you show tension in your fingers?

Then show them the film again and encourage them to look as closely as they can at the camera angles. If they had to take photographs of four main points in this one-minute clip, where would they be?

Allow the children time to work on their four moments. The camera person is also working as director, so they need to give clear instructions. Encourage them to think carefully about where they are taking their photographs – the wrong background can completely destroy the integrity of their finished piece. If appropriate, allow the children to use outdoor settings. If you find that you need to work indoors, you might find it useful to have a selection of drapes at the ready; they can provide an instant disguise for things like climbing frames and can provide a dramatic backdrop.

Step 4: Putting the work together and interacting with it

You can import the photographs that the children have produced on any sort of program that will allow them to present a running slide show of images – PowerPoint, Textease or Photostory 3 are examples of programs that will allow you to do this quickly and simply.

There are many ways of developing what you have – the children can add pages of text to explain the story (just like in the book) or you could record voice-overs. A really exciting thing to do is to encourage the children to interact with their own pictures. Theatre is increasingly using still and moving images as part of the drama on stage. Sometimes characters literally step out of films and onto the stage. Have two copies of the last image that each group has produced (the cliff-hanger). One copy should be blown up onto A3 for the group to look at, the other should be copied onto acetate, ready to be displayed on an overhead projector. Explain to the children that you are going to project their photograph onto the wall. They are going to freeze in front of it, as if they belong to the photograph itself and then simultaneously burst into action, making the picture come to life. To begin with, ask the children to study the A3 picture and make the still image again. They then need to work out how they can move from this position and burst into some live action which should last no more than ten seconds. They should then freeze into one final still image.

When the children have done this, tell them that each group is going to step out of their real picture and show the rest of the class their action. Choose a group to go first and project their image onto a wall where there is enough room for them to step and move in front. Make sure that the overhead is far enough back so that they are not in danger of running into it.

This will be as exciting to watch as it will be to act. Using the ideas in the book as an inspiration, children will have pieced together moments of frozen drama and snippets of fast action. The last activity will work as a powerful finale to the imaginative work they have developed together.

Guidance for assessment

Any assessment of this work will be related back to the Key learning for drama, which stated that by the end of this unit, the children will have:

- collaborated in pairs to create a sound and a movement to represent a clockwork toy – *how effectively do the children make the movements? Are they definite and clear? How well do they co-ordinate the sound and the movement?*
- moved into a whole-class representation of clockwork – *how disciplined are the children when they move into a larger group? How well do they use the space? How effectively do they link the movements?*

- collaborated in groups to make decisions about the Great Invention and to produce a short piece of drama with words – *how well are they able to participate in a group? Are they able to listen to other people's opinions? Do they make suggestions? How effective is the final piece? Does it tell the story clearly?*
- collaborated in groups to change movements into still images to be photographed – *do the children adapt their ideas after direction? Are they emphasising their actions and holding them in strong positions? Have they chosen camera shots that focus on small details as well as larger ones?*
- collaborated in groups to move from a still image to a short piece of moving action – *how controlled are the children when holding the first still image and do they recognise the right point to move from still to moving image? Are the children able to finish the action and move into the final still image together as a group?*

Adapting this unit

Graphic novels like *Hugo Cabret* are an important element of many children's reading diet. Like this book, many can offer good starting points for image-making, sound and movement work, and filming.

5P | *Sir Gawain and the Green Knight*

This unit is based on *Sir Gawain and the Green Knight*.

Where this unit fits in

In this unit, children will work with the legend *Sir Gawain and the Green Knight* to create a performance that is essentially storytelling in action. The characters speak through the storytellers and, in this performance, every child in the class has their own part of the story to tell.

Sir Gawain and the Green Knight is an Arthurian tale that contains all the key elements that children will recognise in a legend: a hero, conflict, a journey, love, a magical tool and resolution. The full story is told in different steps throughout this unit.

Myths and legends are covered in depth in the *Primary Framework for literacy*. A dramatisation of this story, developed from children's own ideas and responses, will give them a greater insight into the construction of myths and legends, the themes, the types of characters and what makes an English legend different from legends from other countries.

Key learning

Key learning for drama

By the end of this unit, the children will have:

- created notes for, rehearsed and performed stories designed to interest an audience;
- developed a piece of drama through improvisation in pairs, groups and as a whole class;
- adapted and improved a piece of drama for performance;
- performed in front of an audience.

Primary Framework for literacy objectives

- Speaking – tell a story using notes designed to cue techniques such as repetition, recap and humour.
- Group discussion and interaction – understand the process of decision-making.
- Drama – perform a scripted scene making use of dramatic conventions; use and recognise the impact of theatrical effects in drama.

Resources

- A version of the story. (The one we used for this unit was taken from www.myths.e2bn.org which includes animated clips of the legends themselves as well as other printable resources for teachers.)
- A round table and a rectangular table with chairs.
- Two crowns – one each for Arthur and Guinevere.
- Medieval-style music to be played in the background of certain scenes.
- A clear rehearsal space, with the opportunity to do some rehearsal in the space where it will be performed.

Steps for teaching and learning

Step 1: Setting the scene – King Arthur's Court

The story begins with a feast at Christmastide when all the Knights of the Round Table are gathered around King Arthur.

The first part of the play should capture the lively atmosphere of an Arthurian banquet. Set up the room so the children walk in to find a round table surrounded by chairs in the centre of the hall, with appropriate music playing in the background.

The characters of Arthur, Guinevere, Gawain and the Green Knight can be picked out of a hat. In this play they will not actually have any lines to say, but their positioning in the Court scenes will be important. Divide the rest of the class into five groups, assigning character types to each group: Knights, musicians, servants, jesters, ladies.

Explain to the children that they are going to be making a still image of King Arthur's Court, frozen in time as if sewn into a tapestry. The round table is where the Knights will sit. The children can step into the still image individually or in pairs. The image they create might connect with another person; this might include someone pouring a drink for someone, or carrying in one half of something long or heavy.

Discuss the importance of where to place the characters. They should not block other people and, as much as possible, facial expressions should be facing the front, just as they would in a tapestry or painting. Examples of medieval tapestry that might inform this image are easy enough to find online.

Step 2: Bringing the Court to life

Explain that as soon as the music starts, the still image is going to come to life and at this point each character should interact with someone from another group. To practise, tell the children that as soon as the music starts they have just 30 seconds to find another character to speak to, and they must do this in role. Remind them that they can talk to each other in groups as well as pairs.

After 30 seconds, stop the children by turning down the music. Discuss what might have been improved. Then tell them that, this time, the scene is going to take up to one minute. They must keep reacting throughout and communicate with as many different characters as possible. Attendants will behave very differently with each other than they do with King Arthur and the Knights, and vice versa. Discuss this, and explain how you should see this in their improvisation.

Step 3: The entrance of the Green Knight

It is into this jubilant atmosphere that the mysterious Green Knight will make his entrance. So, to create dramatic impact, the children will need to make sure there is a contrast between the opening festivities in the scene and the moment he silences the Knights.

Choose a child to play the Green Knight. When, and only when, he passes them, they should fall silent and watch him carefully. The silence should not be instant, but should sweep gradually through the Court.

Step 4: The Green Knight challenges the Knights

Tell the children the first part of the story:

At first the Knights of the Round Table assume that the Green Knight has come in looking for a fight or a battle, but his challenge is actually very different. He wants the Knights to prove whether they are truly courageous. He tells them that he would like them to take a blow at him with his axe on condition that in a year and a day, he will do the same to them. To begin with, King Arthur offers to take up the challenge, but the young

Sir Gawain quickly intercedes, feeling that the King should not be compromised in this way. Gawain is reluctant to take a blow at the Knight, taking his time over the deed, and before he raises the axe, promises to find the Knight in a year and day. Eventually Gawain chops right through the Knight's neck, beheading him. To the amazement of the Knights and all in the room, the Green Knight simply picks up his head and reminds Gawain not to forget to seek him out.

Ask the children to move back into their groups. Between them, they must tell the story from their character's point of view, each group having a different part to tell. There are many ways of splitting up this part of the story, but you might choose:

- Knights – a description of the Knight;
- ladies – the Knight offering his challenge;
- minstrels – how King Arthur's Knights responded to the challenge;
- servants – Sir Gawain takes the blow and promises to return in a year and a day;
- jesters – the Green Knight picks up his head and reminds them all of the final part of the challenge.

Emphasise that the story must be told in the style of their characters. For example, the musicians may tell the story with simple accompaniment in the background. The servants may enjoy gossiping about how uncourageous the Knights were when the mysterious man first offered his challenge. The minstrels and the Knights may emphasise the courage of King Arthur's warriors, whereas the jesters will pick up on the humour in the situation, going to great lengths to describe how ridiculous it looked when the Green Knight picked up his own head.

Give each group a piece of flip-chart paper and some marker pens where they can make simple notes to guide them in their story (model an example before they start). You may wish to assign specific roles within the group to make sure that everyone is engaged in the task. As well as a scribe you may have two or three children as story-writers, a questioner who makes sure that everyone is involved, asking helpful questions to a child who may not have offered any ideas for a while, and a final decision-maker, who listens to the ideas and has the final say on which elements should be used (rather like an editor).

Step 5: Threading the stories together

Sometimes it might be appropriate for one character to speak; sometimes, when greater emphasis is needed, the whole group may speak together. At times, they might want the story to sound like a conversation so there may be interplay between the characters. It is important to remember that each group has only a short section of the story; its delivery should take no more than a minute per group. Allow the children plenty of rehearsal time to try this out. It is helpful to assign a director to each group who will pay as much attention to how the scene will look as to how it sounds.

Step 6: Presenting the stories on stage

The children should now practise moving from the positions that they were in when the Green Knight entered the Court, to a position where each group can tell their part of the story. They may decide to remain scattered and tell the story from different positions – this can look very effective. Other groups may decide to move together as a group.

Step 7: Creating the journey

> Sir Gawain has to embark on a treacherous journey to seek out the place of the Green Knight: the Green Chapel.

This part of the story can be created effectively through group sounds and movement. Each group will provide a different obstacle for Sir Gawain on his journey which might include:

- bears;
- wolves;
- a swamp;
- dark shadows;
- a forest.

Sir Gawain will spend no more than about 30 seconds with each group, so the movements they decide to make must be carefully choreographed. Ask the children to think carefully about which props they might want to use to heighten the effect. For example, to create a swamp, the children may wish to lie on the floor with dark cloths draped over the top of them which they can move slowly with their arms and bodies as the Knight walks through them. To create mysterious shadows, the children may choose to turn all the lights off and shine torches in different directions.

Decide as a class how these obstacles will be arranged. For example, will they be set out side-by-side in a horizontal line across the stage or will Sir Gawain twist in and out of them?

Step 8: The castle

Eventually Sir Gawain sees a castle where he decides to take some rest because he has been travelling for several days.

This scene can begin as a repeat of the first scene at King Arthur's Court, but there should be slight differences. The table where the Lord and his family sit should appear different, for example this table could be rectangular rather than round.

The children will begin by creating the same sort of atmosphere as they did in the first scene, so go through the same process, producing a whole-class still image, bringing it gradually to life. However, when Sir Gawain enters the scene, the atmosphere should be different from when the Green Knight entered Arthur's castle. When Sir Gawain enters, the Court of this new castle should quieten down rather than go silent. The point of this is that Sir Gawain is warmly welcomed by the Lord of the Castle, a contrast to the experience of the Green Knight.

Step 9: Sir Gawain and the Lady of the Castle

Sir Gawain is warmly welcomed by his host who is very good to him. After three days, he says he must leave to seek out the Green Chapel, but his host assures him that it is very near and there is no need to leave just yet. He then tells him that he is going hunting and will bring him back a gift in exchange for whatever Sir Gawain receives in the castle. Sir Gawain is confused by this, but thanks his host.

While his host is away, he is visited by the Lady of the Castle, who is very attracted to Sir Gawain. He rejects her, but she will not go until she has given him a kiss. The Lord of the Castle returns with venison which he presents to Sir Gawain as promised. Sir Gawain thanks him with an embrace and a kiss, so giving his host the one thing he had received that day in the castle. The next day, the same thing happens. The Lord of the Castle returns with a bear and a goose which is received with an embrace and a two kisses – Sir Gawain had again refused the advances of the Lady of the Castle, but had accepted two kisses. On the third day he refused her advances one more time, but this time accepted three kisses and a magic girdle which she claimed would protect whoever wore it from any weapon. That evening the Lord brought back a foul fox skin which he said was a poor reward for the three kisses that Sir Gawain had offered him. It was time to go.

Now it is time for the children to be storytellers again. Again, give each group a different part of the story. For example:

• the host welcomes Sir Gawain to the castle and shows him great kindness;

- the Lady of the Castle's attraction to Sir Gawain;
- the events of the first day;
- the events of the second day;
- the events of the third day.

The servants will enjoy gossiping about what has gone on in secret between Sir Gawain and the Lady of the House. The minstrels may tell of how strong and noble Sir Gawain has been to reject the beautiful woman. The jesters will find it hilarious that Sir Gawain is so embarrassed and has to keep giving the Lord of the House kisses because it is all he has received.

Again, give the children the opportunity to rehearse how their stories will be presented. Expect them to use different techniques at different points in the story.

Step 10: Sir Gawain leaves the castle

Finally, it is time for Sir Gawain to leave. His journey is hazardous. For this part of the story, the children can repeat what they developed in Step 7 when they created obstacles for Sir Gawain to move through. Repetition works well in stories and is certainly a feature of many myths and legends, particularly when they have been developed into narrative or epic poems.

Step 11: Sir Gawain arrives at the mouth of a large cave

The Green Knight emerges from this dark place, his head firmly back on his shoulders. He challenges Sir Gawain to complete his side of the bargain. Bravely, the young Knight takes off his helmet and exposes his neck. At first when the axe is raised he flinches – the Green Knight mocks him for this. He declares that the next time he will not flinch. The axe is lifted again, without being dropped down to make a blow. Sir Gawain insists that the Green Knight get on with making the strike. The Knight demands that Gawain is patient. The third time the axe is lifted up into the air and dropped onto Gawain's neck. To his great surprise and relief, he finds that he is unharmed, apart from a few drops of blood. Then he discovers that he is not standing before the Green Knight but the Lord of the Castle who commends him for his bravery. He explains that he sent his wife to test whether he was a man of true honour. The drops of blood he received were for the girdle which he was given in the castle and did not give to the Lord in return for the fox skin. Sir Gawain offers the girdle to his host, who tells him that he must keep it; Sir Gawain continues to wear it as a reminder that he should never become too arrogant about his bravery. The Knight introduces himself as Sir Berblake.

This is the last part of the story that the children will tell. Again, split this up into different sections:

- ladies – a description of the cave;
- servants – the axe is raised for the first time;
- minstrels – the axe is raised for the second time;
- Knights – the axe is raised for the third time;
- jesters – the Knight reveals his true identity.

This time, two of the children will mime the action between Sir Gawain and the Green Knight, and the others will be storytellers.

Step 12: Sir Gawain returns to Camelot

For this final scene, the children can repeat what they did in the first scene, creating a 'tapestry picture' that comes to life when the music starts. When Sir Gawain enters, silence can sweep through the group once more, finishing the play with one last still image dotted with expectant faces who want to hear the Knight's amazing story of survival.

Guidance on assessment

Any assessment of this work will be related back to the Key learning for drama, which stated that by the end of this unit the children will have:

- created notes for, rehearsed and performed stories designed to interest an audience – *in rehearsal have the children adapted their notes to make improvements to their performance? Do their notes make a difference to their performance?*
- developed a piece of drama through improvisation in groups and as a whole class – *how well do children transfer improvisation in small groups to a drama performance as part of a whole class?*
- adapted and improved a piece of drama for performance – *how effectively do children play their role on stage? How well do they stay in character?*

Adapting this unit

This kind of storytellers' theatre can be used with all kinds of stories. For a really good example of the technique in professional theatre, show the children an extract from the RSC's production of *Nicholas Nickleby* which is available on DVD.

Leon and the Place Between

This unit is based on *Leon and the Place Between*, by Angela McAllister and Grahame Baker-Smith, Templar, ISBN 978-1-840-11801-8.

Where this unit fits in

The vibrancy of the language and the interesting, sometimes surreal illustrations in this picture book will challenge and inspire Year 6. The story itself is very simple. A family go to the circus, thrilled at the prospect of seeing a famous magician who can make things disappear. Leon is more reluctant than the rest of his family because, to begin with, he doesn't believe in magic. It is he who ends up being called onto the stage and, after being made to disappear, travels to 'The Place Between'. This turns out to be where magicians send the things that they have made invisible. These 'things' (living or otherwise) remain in the mysterious place until they are called back.

This story can be used as a stimulus for writing an advert about a circus which is coming to town. In this unit, the children will gather the ideas to prepare them for writing an advert for a circus, inspired by the text and the drama they create. They will also create an instant performance poem.

The illustrations in the book are so rich and unusual that there is a lot of potential for using the book as a stimulus for art work. The pictures are created using computer generation, collage using everyday objects, photographs and paintings. Linking Art to ICT in this way is a very interesting way of working.

Key learning

Key learning for drama

By the end of this unit, the children will have:

- worked collaboratively to create instant images, communicating only through gesture;
- explored the language of circus posters;
- created their own circus acts through still and moving images;
- recorded and used some of the descriptive language they developed through drama.

Primary Framework for literacy objectives

- Speaking – use the techniques of dialogic talk to explore ideas, topics or issues.
- Drama – improvise using a range of drama strategies and conventions to explore themes such as hopes, fears and desires; consider the overall impact of a live or recorded performance, identifying dramatic ways of conveying characters' ideas and building tension.
- Understand and interpret texts – appraise a text quickly, deciding on its value, quality or usefulness; understand underlying themes, causes and points of view.

Steps for teaching and learning

Step 1: The circus is coming!

The first texts anyone encounters before the circus arrives in town are the advertising posters that inform everyone of its impending arrival. Drama can help children to develop rich descriptions that can be used on their own posters.

The titles of circus acts are like miniature adverts in themselves; the wording has to be carefully chosen to reflect the spirit of the entertainers.

This can be explored through a simple game of 'Make me a ... ' Children need to be organised into groups of threes or fours. The teacher will call out 'Make me a ... ' and each group will respond by creating a still image of the description. The added challenge is that the children are not allowed to speak to each other. They must only communicate through gesture. Begin by asking them to create some simple things such as a circle, a straight line, a comma or a full stop. Then develop into more complex ideas; these can include the names of circus acts.

These are just some suggestions for circus titles. Many more can be accessed through an Internet search:

- Flying Valentino;
- Goldie the Wonder Horse;
- Carmencita, the lovely star of the trapeze;
- The Bouncing Caballeros, stars of the trampoline;
- Little Alan, the comedy bombshell;
- The Waddling Wonders.

After each example, ask the whole class to relax from their image, and choose one particular group to re-form so that everyone can look closely at their ideas. You might ask questions such as:

- What shapes can you see in this image?
- Look at the expression of this character. Put it on yourself. Can you describe what each part of your face is doing?
- How do you think they want the audience to feel? How can you tell?

The children might say things like, 'My eyes are staring sharply into space', 'My lips are tightly sealed', 'There is a deep line across my forehead', and so on. All of these descriptions give away small points about how the characters are feeling, and they focus on action rather than saying directly *how* the character is feeling or what they might be thinking. Concentrating on this not only challenges the children to think deeply about their description, but it also fine-tunes their acting; they learn more and more about how the face and body has its own language on stage.

Step 2: The acts

Organise the children into groups of three or four and ask them to create their own circus act. They must display the act as a single still image, paying careful attention to the overall shape it creates. If it was to be photographed for a billboard, how could it be made to look interesting?

Once they have done this, ask them to think of their own name for the act. Remind them of the qualities they identified in the names of circus acts in the 'Make me a ... ' game. Make your expectations clear. Will you expect to see examples of word play or alliteration, for example? Will you want the children to use polysyllabic words so that the titles become almost like lists of spectacular sounding syllables?

Give out pieces of A4 paper and large marker pens so that children can write down the name of the act in big letters. Immediately you have a number of acts that children can list on their posters, all showing an awareness of the right style of language to use. Carefully collect them in so they can be used in the next stage.

Step 3: Moving and making tableaux

Spread all the circus acts face down on the floor. If you want to, you can also include some of the acts that you showed at the beginning. Make sure there is plenty of space around each one because the children are going to be walking around them in their groups.

Play some circus music. Explain that while the music plays, the children are going to walk around the room, taking on the role of their performers as if they were walking around the floor of the big top, ready to perform. When the music stops, they should stop by the nearest piece of paper. Then, when prompted, they turn this over and think of a tableau for the title of the act. Give them about two minutes to do this. Ask them to make sure they remember their tableau, and where the paper is positioned because they will need to return to it later on.

Play the music again and encourage them to move around until the music stops and they are standing at a different piece of paper. Again, when prompted, they turn the paper over and make a tableau of the act. Repeat this twice more so that the children end up with four tableaux of different circus acts at four different points in the room.

The next step is to get the children to practise walking from each of these four points to another. Use a musical instrument like a maraca to signal when you want them to move. Each time a short shaking sound is made, the children move to the next point and stop, waiting to hear another short shake. Playfully catch the children out in different ways. For example, establish a good rhythm, then break it by making a shaking sound at an unexpected moment. Get the children moving quite quickly, then, without warning, make the pause between the sounds much longer. This develops children's awareness of being 'in the moment' during a performance, being completely alert to the signals around them so they are ready to respond appropriately. They should move from point one, to two, to three, to four, back to one and so on. Eventually you can remove the titles from the floor.

Step 4: Adding music

Now the children can create their own exciting circus spectacle by forming the appropriate tableau each time they stop at one of the four spaces. This time, play circus music in the background, but again, signal the point to move by playing a clear sound on a musical instrument. After a short shake sound, the children move to their first point, form their tableau and hold it, until they hear the sound signal once more. Then they will move on to the next point, and so on. This will create a dynamic scene where children will feel as though they are immersed in a circus atmosphere.

Step 5: Building language

Now the children have moved around the titles, spread them out onto the floor once more. This is an opportunity to capture some good language. Modern advertising posters or leaflets for a circus will not just list titles, but they will also describe the type of action that might be seen. Encourage the children to stop once more at each of their titles and spread out some more words around it, describing what they conveyed in their tableaux. For example, the 'Tenacious Tightrope Twins' might have around them words such as 'danger', 'absolute control', 'scaling unfathomable heights' and so on. Through the drama, the children are able to build up a useful word bank of ideas which can be translated into a piece of extended writing.

Step 6: The battle of the magicians

All circus posters put a big emphasis on 'the main attraction'. The story really helps us with this, because the main attraction is the magician. A good way of exploring his character is to play a 'battle of the magicians' game.

When Leon, the main character in the story, is called onto the stage, the magician makes him disappear. He travels to the 'Place Between', discovering that it contains a myriad of curiosities and living things that remain there because they have not been called back by the magician.

In pairs, the children can work like battling magicians confronting one another, each trying to out-do the other by calling back the things they have left in 'The Place Between'. As one person calls something back, the other has to take it out of the bag and decide what to do with it. For example, child one might call out 'White rabbit'. Child two might mime taking the rabbit out by the ears, carrying it away and then carefully setting it down on the ground to hop away. Child two might then come back and call out 'A banana jelly'. Child one will mime taking the wobbling jelly out of the bag and perhaps take out an imaginary spoon and start to eat it.

Then give the children a piece of paper and a pen. Allow them one minute to list as many examples of what could be found in the 'Place Between' as possible. Emphasise that, at this point, they should not worry too much about spelling; it is a good quantity of ideas that is important. They need not stick to the ones that they acted out, they can add new ideas which might include some that they have heard being used around them.

Step 7: The 'Place Between'

Now the children have nearly enough information to create an advertising poster for the circus in the story. But what would really make an impact on the poster would be a quotation from Leon, someone who had really travelled to the 'Place Between' and could describe what is was like. The children will work creatively and imaginatively to develop this quotation.

Ask the children to move into groups of three or four, positioned around the outside of the room. In the centre, place a hat – the doorway to the 'Place Between'. One child from each group goes up to the hat, looks inside and returns to the group.

Obviously, what is inside the hat is entirely dependent on the children's imaginations. The other members of the group are allowed to ask a question each about what the land is like. Emphasise that the children cannot be wrong. They must trust that the questions will help the story to develop and their ideas may sound ordinary to start with but, gradually, a story will emerge.

When they have done this, the next person in each group goes to look in the hat. The stories should keep building on what has gone before. This challenges the children to think creatively; each child who tells what they see is helped and steered by the questions asked. When all the children have had an opportunity to look at the hat, ask them to think carefully about all of their ideas. They are going to use the ideas to produce a quotation from Leon describing the 'Place Between' in exactly 20 words.

Once completed, ask the children to sit in a circle and ask each group to read out their quotation. The other children in the room can ask any questions they like and the group has to respond to them as instantaneously as possible.

Step 8: Making posters

Throughout these drama sessions, you have been able to bring the circus atmosphere into the classroom. The children have been acting as writers, gathering snippets of ideas, sharing them in spoken and written words, and learning from texts they have seen. All the children's notes should be saved, even typed up, so that when the teacher does a whole-class writing session where an advert is modelled for the children, it is possible to draw on the ideas developed through drama.

Guidance on assessment

Any assessment of this work will be related back to the Key learning for drama, which stated that by the end of this unit the children will have:

- worked collaboratively to create instant images, communicating only through gesture – *how successfully do the children communicate their ideas without words? Do any of the children show strong leadership? Are they able to work as a team?*
- explored the language of circus posters – *are the children transferring the ideas they have seen on the posters to their drama and written work?*

- created their own circus acts through still and moving images – *how well-choreographed are these sequences? How controlled are the children's gestures? How successfully do they work as a team?*
- recorded and used some of the descriptive language they developed through drama – *is this reflected in their final writing?*

Adapting this unit

Although the book and its ideas are quite complex, the world of the circus, its performers and the language used to describe them will appeal to all ages in the 7–11 range.

6C | Shipwrecked

Making for survival

Where this unit fits in

There are many stories about shipwrecks, from *The Tempest* to *Robinson Crusoe* to Michael Morpurgo's *Kensuke's Kingdom*. They have a strong appeal to children of this age, allowing them to explore ideas not just about survival in an unknown and hostile environment, but also about how they might cooperate and work together. Building on these ideas, this unit has strong links to technology and geography, focusing on mapping the island, building shelters, and devising ways of collecting water and providing food. It also has strong elements of Personal, Social and Health Education by developing the idea of a group of survivors who need to cooperate and find ways of living and working together. The suggestions in this unit give a broad overall structure, but the eventual direction the drama takes will be very dependent on the children's ideas and responses.

Key learning

Key learning for drama

By the end of this unit, the children will have:

* worked together to create a storm through sound and movement;
* created still and moving images to show arrival and exploration of an unknown island;

119

- collaborated to create a shared image/map of the island;
- created a form of meeting and decision-making, and followed the agreed rules in role;
- worked in role to explore some of the issues, tensions and conflicts of living together.

Primary Framework for literacy objectives

- Speaking – use a range of oral techniques to present persuasive arguments.
- Group discussion and interaction – consider examples of conflict and resolution, exploring the language used.
- Drama – improvise using a range of drama strategies and conventions to explore themes such as hopes, fears and desires.

Resources

- Various materials for building the shelter(s) in Step 3. This might include some bamboo poles and canes, cloths, rope and string, and perhaps a camouflage net (a very versatile resource that can be bought from most army surplus stores).
- A large sheet of paper for making the map in Step 4 (rolls of thick paper used under carpets are cheaply available from DIY stores).
- Various natural materials for Step 5 – exactly what is needed will depend on the ideas children have for what to make, but they will need to depend on what might be naturally available on the island.

Steps for teaching and learning

Step 1: Creating a storm through sound and movement

It can be useful to begin this work by looking for pictures and video of storms at sea on the Internet – a quick search will turn up all sorts that can stimulate children's thinking. Then focus on the sounds you would expect to hear if you were at sea in such a storm. Experiment not only with non-verbal sounds of wind and waves, but also using the words themselves (crashing, roaring, splitting, ripping, etc.) to create a whole-class soundscape. In groups of three or four, get the children to create four tableaux of the storm. These might be literal interpretations of, for example, people struggling to control the sails of a ship, or they might be more abstract representations of sea, wind and waves. Next, ask the children to create linking movements between their tableaux and develop them into strong, powerful motifs. As they practise and repeat these movements, they will hold their tableaux for less and less time until they create a continuous and repeating sequence of movement. Then experiment with ways of combining the sound and the movement. You might do this by the children performing both 'live' (perhaps adding some extra recorded music to heighten the effect), or you might record your soundscape and play it over the movement.

Step 2: Washed ashore

Working in their groups, ask the children to create images in the form of still–move–still to show the survivors of the storm being washed ashore on an island. They begin by creating one tableau, then a second, then a few moments of movement and sound between the two. Rather than looking at each group's work in turn, get all the groups to perform them at the same time and ask them to hold the final still when they have finished. When they are all still and silent, narrate:

> You are the only survivors of the storm, washed up on an uninhabited island. The ship is completely lost and, with it, all supplies of food and fresh water. You will need to work together to find shelter, water and food. No one can know how long you will be here.

Then ask the children to relax, sit and discuss what might happen next. It is worth noticing that there is no specific information about time or place, why they were on the ship or where it was going: some of these ideas will emerge as the drama develops. But you may need to remind the children that the island is uninhabited and deliberately steer them away from ideas of pirates, cannibals or even aliens from outer space!

Step 3: Building a shelter

The survivors will need to build some kind of shelter to keep them warm, safe and dry. This could be done in the hall using cloths, PE equipment and any other materials you have available. Or you might make a representation of the shelter in the corner of the classroom. If possible, though, take the children out into the school grounds, provide them with a range of resources and work together to create a full-size version of the shelter that the survivors might build. After they have worked on their shelter(s), talk about the ideas they came up with, how the shelters might stand up to various weather conditions and how different groups cooperated to produce them.

Step 4: Mapping the island

Ask the groups to create tableaux of the survivors exploring their island. Take time to look at each group's work and ask the rest of the class to discuss what they think it might show. As you review each group's work, shared ideas about the island and what it is like will emerge. These can then be combined to create a whole-class map of the island. Seat the children round a large sheet of paper. Using one large pen, a child draws the section of coastline which is immediately in front of them, then passes the pen on to the next child who draws the next section – as the pen passes round the whole class, an entire outline of the island emerges. It can be very helpful if the children are encouraged to stay silent and not comment as the outline of the island emerges. Once the outline is drawn, groups can be given more pens and asked to add details to the map based on the information they showed in their tableaux.

Once they have created their imagined island, the class can talk about where the sources of food and water might be, and what sorts of technologies will be needed to collect, hunt and gather.

122

Step 5: What do they need to make?

This is a good opportunity to design and make a number of things
that the survivors will need on the island. How will they collect and
carry water? Will they hunt and/or trap animals for food? Will they
catch fish? How will they prepare and cook the food safely? What
about ways of signalling to passing ships and aircraft? Once children
have come up with a number of ideas, they can work in pairs or small
groups either to make the actual objects, or working models of them
that they can share with the rest of the class. Much of this designing
and making will take place in other curriculum time, but the drama
will provide a meaningful context and purpose for it. It will also
provide a valuable opportunity for children to consolidate much of
their learning about practical designing and making, and their
understanding about food.

Step 6: Meeting together and making decisions

Talk about how and where the survivors might meet. What sorts of
things do they need to discuss? How is their meeting organised? Who
gets to speak? How do they arrive at decisions? The children should
have plenty of ideas about these questions. If, for example, they have
experienced 'circle time' at school, they may suggest an object that is
held to signify whose turn it is to speak. You can practise the form of
the meeting by using it for pairs and groups to present their ideas from
the previous step, demonstrating how the survivors might collect food
and water, prepare and cook food safely. Everyone has the chance to
comment on other people's designs and ideas, but they must do so
within the agreed rules of the meeting. Even at this stage you may get
some disagreement about what they should eat, whether they should
hunt for food, or whether they should catch and eat the fish.

Step 7: Introducing a dilemma

By now, you and the class will have built in some detail a shared story
of the island and the survivors who find themselves there. At this

stage in the story, life might settle into a daily pattern of work and rest, gathering and preparing food, perhaps signalling to potential rescuers. If, as the teacher, you are prepared to take a role in the drama yourself, you can introduce a dilemma into the story which will take it to another, deeper level and extend thinking further.

Set up the meeting and, remembering to abide by its rules yourself, tell the other survivors that you are growing more and more concerned about the impact you are all having on the island. Tell the meeting that you have heard reports that many of the fruits and berries on which you depend for your food are getting harder to find. Those survivors who fish say that there are fewer and fewer of them and that they are having to go farther and farther to catch them. There are already signs that numbers of some of the animals being taking for food are declining. What should they do? What responsibility do they have for looking after the island? How can they balance that responsibility with the need to eat and survive? As they explore these questions, children will be touching on some of the major ecological and environmental issues which often concern them greatly. In this instance, though, you have presented them in an accessible and manageable form, allowing them to debate and make decisions that they can follow through within the context of the drama.

Depending on the decisions that the children make in their roles as survivors, you may choose to introduce a further conflict. Narrate that, as the survivors have taken more care of the island and its ecology, food has been in shorter supply and has been carefully rationed so that everyone gets an equal share. But one of them has been caught stealing extra food. It is a good idea to take the role of the thief yourself, allowing the rest of the class to explore the issue without creating an 'outsider'. You can be called before the meeting to explain what you have done and the others will decide what action to take against you. It is important that you give your role a name that is not your own and make it clear that you and the role you play are two different people. You may need to stress that the survivors are deciding what to do with someone who has broken the rules, not the class deciding what to do with their teacher. If you want to challenge their thinking further, you might tell them that you took the food for a member of your family who is sick and needs extra food to get well again.

Step 8: How will the story end?

By researching factual examples and by exploring a number of stories through their reading, children will discover that shipwreck stories can end in a number of ways. The survivors may be rescued (as, for example, in *Robinson Crusoe* or *Kensuke's Kingdom*), or they may live on the island and have children there (as with the descendants of HMS *Bounty* on Pitcairn Island). When they have had the chance to explore and talk about possibilities, ask groups to present their suggested endings as either a short scene or a series of three or four linked tableaux that tell the end of the story. As they review each other's work, the children can comment on and discuss the possible outcomes – which might be most likely, which might make the 'best' ending.

As a final activity, ask groups to create either a single captioned tableau or a still–move–still that captures something of what the survivors have learned from their experience. These final images will stimulate further discussion about learning to live together, dealing with conflict and overcoming challenges.

Linking to writing

As this unit of work develops, it will offer plenty of opportunities for children to write. Most obviously, they can keep a journal or diary that can be updated after each drama lesson. Encourage them to write in role as one of the survivors, detailing not only the events that take place, but also the ways that they feel about them. Some of these extracts can be read aloud over some of the drama – for example, the tableaux of coming ashore in Step 2 – to explore the contrasts between outward appearances and actions and inner thoughts and feelings.

125

Guidance on assessment

Any assessment of this work will be related back to the Key learning for drama, which stated that by the end of this unit the children will have:

- worked together to create a storm through sound and movement – *who offers imaginative and original ideas? Who is deliberate and controlled in the performance?*
- created still and moving images to show arrival and exploration of an unknown island – *by this stage children should be creating tableaux and moving images that are very precise and show that they have thought about details of movement, posture and facial expression; how evident is this in their images?*
- collaborated to create a shared image/map of the island – *how much do the children build on each other's ideas to create a map and images that show a genuine collaboration?*
- created a form of meeting and decision-making and followed the agreed rules in role – *who makes suggestions for this? Who contributes in the meeting? Do they keep to their own agreed rules?*
- worked in role to explore some of the issues, tensions and conflicts of living together – *do they stay in role as the discussions, tensions and conflicts develop? Are their contributions consistent with the unfolding story?*

Adapting this unit

Because it is written with older children in mind, some of the elements and key ideas in this unit are quite complex and demanding. But the overall structure could readily be used with younger children – the idea of finding an island, settling on it and working out how to live together will have a wide appeal.

6F Silent film

This unit is based on Charlie Chaplin's *The Circus*, 1928.

Where this unit fits in

The films of Charlie Chaplin continue to surprise and delight film enthusiasts of today, even though most were created over 70 years ago. Even today, his performances appear fresh and ingenious; *The Circus* is a brilliant example of his extraordinary talent. Throughout this film, Chaplin recognises the comic potential in simple everyday situations, crafting from these a series of mini narratives which include their own introduction, conflict and resolution. By taking a simple idea like this, children can create very high-quality short silent movies that teach them as much about physical expression as they do about good storytelling. They can learn a lot about how to communicate through their faces and bodies, without using any words at all.

The film has a simple plot. Chaplin plays a tramp who wanders along to the circus in the hope of finding some good luck amongst the crowds. While he is there, he falls in love with a trapeze artist who is the daughter of the circus owner. She is ill-treated by her father, and the tramp tries to help her in any way he can, eventually getting a job in the circus as a props man. This proves to be a real hit for the audience because he is so accident-prone that he causes havoc every time he carries anything onto the stage. The circus owner quickly recognises his potential and turns this into an act. The little tramp becomes a clown and as a result the big top has a full house every night.

However, all does not run smoothly for him: the trapeze artist falls in love with a tall, handsome tightrope walker. Because of her ill treatment, the trapeze artist runs away from the circus. The little tramp recognises that the only way to improve the situation is for his beloved trapeze artist to marry the man she loves. He speaks to his rival, who happily agrees to marry her. The circus owner is thrilled by what has happened, and there is much joy as the circus caravan leaves town. But not for the little tramp, who walks in the opposite direction, alone again.

To help your class to produce a really effective, high-quality piece of film, this unit does not focus on creating a long story. It focuses in on key moments in the film that may last only a couple of minutes but can be closely analysed and used as an inspiration for their own work. By the end of these sessions, your children will have produced very short pieces of work, but they will have learnt much about acting, storytelling and how to speak to an audience through a camera.

Key learning

Key learning for drama

By the end of this unit, the children will have:

- created short scenes through improvisation;
- collaborated in groups, taking on different roles;
- experimented with the genre of silent film;
- created a short film inspired by scenes in *The Circus*;
- created a shot for a movie poster.

Primary Framework for literacy objectives

- Speaking – use the techniques of dialogic talk to explore ideas, topics or issues.

- Group discussion and interaction – consider examples of conflict and resolution; understand and use a variety of ways to criticise constructively and respond to criticism.
- Drama – improvise using a range of drama strategies and conventions to explore themes such as hopes, fears and desires; devise a performance considering how to adapt it for a specific audience; consider the overall impact of a live or recorded performance, identifying dramatic ways of conveying characters' ideas and building tension.

Resources

- A DVD of Charlie Chaplin's *The Circus*. It is easy to purchase this over the Internet.
- A large uncluttered space would be very useful, such as a hall. Within this space the children need to be able to watch extracts of *The Circus* at different points in your lessons.
- Cameras for recording still and moving images – enough for every group of four in your class. These could be digital cameras that take video clips, or one of the packages that are now available, for example the Digital Blue digital movie creator, which includes editing software that allows you to turn your films into black and white.
- Enough hats for each group of four children.

Steps for teaching and learning

Step 1: Improvising from the film

Before any of the filming begins, it is important to decide who is going to watch the film and why the children are going to create it. Perhaps you could turn the local village or community hall into a cinema one evening, inviting parents and other members of the community to an evening of silent film. Or you might spend a day turning the classroom into a cinema, showing the films at different times to different classes. Whatever you decide, the prospect of an audience will make the children feel more aware of the need for a performance of high quality.

If your class is going to make their own silent film moment in a similar style to Charlie Chaplin, they will need to see ways of working with carefully chosen rules and constraints. This means that you will need to look closely at several key moments in the film, without it as a whole. The children will want to see the whole film eventually, but to begin with, just introduce them to key moments where narrative can be explored.

Show the moment in the film where the little tramp meets the trapeze artist for the first time. It is the morning and she is very hungry because her father denied her any food the night before because she 'missed the hoop again'. She spies the little tramp walking in with food and encourages him to share; at first he is reluctant because he is very hungry himself. Eventually, he offers her a little bite, then turns away for the slightest fraction of a second. When he turns back he finds that she has eaten the entire piece. Stop the film at this point and ask the children to move into pairs.

Explain to the children that they are going to enact what they think might happen next in the film. Offer them a question and some rules: She has been offered a bite of bread but has eaten the entire roll in one gulp, obviously eating far too quickly on an empty stomach. What might be the consequences of this? When you make your scene:

• you must sit on chairs, side by side;
• you must keep your feet on the floor;
• there should be no physical contact.

Give the children time to explore possibilities and then watch some examples. Don't worry if the acting lacks control at this point: once they start filming their ideas, they will get immediate feedback on how they look on the screen.

Step 2: Introducing a prop and starting filming

Next, tell the children what actually happens, without showing them the film. The actors play around with the simple idea of two people sitting beside each other with hiccups. Sometimes the hiccups are in unison, other times at counterpoint, sometimes predictable, sometimes unexpected. Chaplin's hat proves to be a significant prop in this scene. The children can explore what might happen to it as a result of the hiccups.

Ask the children to move into fours and give themselves a number – one, two, three or four. Ones and twos will be actors, three will be a director and four will be camera person. Give each group a hat between them. Ask the children to make three separate 'hiccupping' shots of no longer than five seconds each. One of these shots needs to be a close-up, and one of them has to involve something happening to the hat. The third shot is entirely their choice. The 'director' needs to watch the shape of the picture very closely, analysing whether the story being created by the actors will be clear enough by the time it has been transferred onto the screen.

As the children are working on this idea, be ready to challenge them to improve their work and, where possible, model what you mean. For example, if the children's actions are not clear enough, act out how it might look better. If their film clips need better editing, model how it could be improved with an example for the whole class.

Step 3: Refining the film

Before the children have finished their work, stop them and show how Chaplin deals with the hiccup scene. Ask the children to observe how the actors make the scene so effective. Most of the action takes place in their eyes and their shoulder movements. Their backs are straight and their bodies very still, which allow the tiniest of sudden gestures to appear dramatic. Emphasise that silent-movie acting does not always depend on larger-than-life gestures, but more

131

on clear, deliberate movements, carefully timed. In light of what they have seen, ask the children to return to their film, watch it and make improvements as necessary. It is important that they stick to the stories they created themselves.

Step 4: Exploring tension

One of the most memorable parts of the film is when Chaplin is trapped in the lion's cage. He stands behind bars with a sleeping lion at one end and himself at the other. His eyes grow wide as his terror increases – he knows that he has to be quiet and still, as the slightest noise or movement could wake the dangerous beast. A tiny dog comes yapping in front of the cage and Chaplin can only gesture with his arms and speak with his eyes through the bars.

Now the children have explored how to tell a story through gesture, set up the next scene for them. Ask them to remain in fours, but this time there needs to be three actors and a camera person who will also act as director. The camera person should be different from the last time around.

Give each group a gym mat which will provide the boundary for the imaginary cage. Explain to the children that someone is trapped inside the cage with a dangerous living thing. The 'thing' doesn't have to be an animal, it could be human or supernatural. This 'thing' is asleep but any noise or movement could make it wake up. Another character comes along, and for some reason, creates a disturbance. The children can decide why.

To begin with, ask the children to create a still image that can be photographed, capturing the most anxious moment. Encourage the camera operator to make sure the actors' faces are telling the story and to make sure that the 'shape' of the shot is interesting to look at.

Later on, when this has been photographed and downloaded, tell the children that this is the shot used for the advertising poster for the film. The children can then insert captions, headings and other information onto the picture.

Step 5: A story in four shots

Following this still image, ask the children to create four moving shots to be filmed and played back. The 'dangerous thing' is not allowed to wake up until the final shot. Just as you did with the hiccupping scene, allow the children to see Chaplin's extract before they finish their work. This will give them the opportunity to make any improvements they feel are necessary.

Step 6: Making their own stories

The final step is for the children to create their own Charlie Chaplin style scenario, to be filmed in a set number of shots. If the children find it difficult to choose, you can also provide some suggestions to get them started – sometimes having this choice can help to stimulate thought and imagination. But it is also very likely that most of the children will be keen to create an idea entirely from scratch. Some suggestions from Chaplin's other films might include:

- a restaurant scene with an indoor and an outdoor where a new waiter gets the two mixed up, creating chaos (*Modern Times*);
- a waiter carries a tray across a lively, crowded dance floor, writhing with twirling bodies. The meal has been ordered by a very impatient gentleman (*Modern Times*);
- a man entertains some onlookers by making his food dance. He pushes a fork into each of the two rolls he is about to eat, turning them into a pair of feet. He makes them ballet dance (*Goldrush*).

When the children have chosen or created their scenario, make sure there are clear rules when the filming takes place. For example, you may ask for four key moments to be recorded in ten short shots, five of which need to be close-ups. You may say that all the filming needs to be done in one small area.

After the children have completed their short films, it is important that they should be screened and celebrated. This will be an ideal opportunity to show the whole film of *The Circus*. The discussion that follows will be a rich analysis of comparisons and contrasts between their own work and the work of a very inspiring artist.

Guidance on assessment

Any assessment of this work will be related back to the Key learning for drama, which stated that by the end of this unit the children will have:

- created short scenes through improvisation – *how well are the children able to express their ideas through gesture? How controlled is their work?*
- collaborated in groups, taking on different roles – *is every child in the group engaged in the activity and confident in their role?*
- experimented with the genre of silent film – *are the children able to make comparisons and contrasts between silent film and the films of today?*
- created short films inspired by scenes in *The Circus* – *how successfully have they been able to transfer what they have learnt from the film to their own work?*
- created a shot for a movie poster – *how successfully does this single shot convey the story and the atmosphere?*

Adapting this unit

Because it is aimed at Year 6, the expectations of relating their work to an example of silent film are very high. But younger children can also enjoy making films in this way. There are plenty of clips of silent film that you can download from the Internet to stimulate children's own work.

6P | *Coriolanus*

This unit is based on *Coriolanus*, by William Shakespeare.

Where this unit fits in

Caius Martius is a warrior of incredible skill. When he fights for his beloved Rome, he is able to defeat the Volsces almost single-handedly, even forcing the retreat of their leader, Tullus Aufidius, a warrior he greatly respects.

In order to receive the accolades that he believes are rightly his, he must be prepared to flatter the Plebeians. Unfortunately, he has little respect for them, believing, quite rightly, that they are easily swayed; one day they will adore him, the next they will see him as their enemy.

Like so much of Shakespeare, this play's themes are very relevant in today's world. The power of the press and media has the ability to change opinions just as the crowd in *Coriolanus* is easily swayed by rhetoric. What really appeals to children is the play's links with celebrity culture – people yearn for fame and adoration yet, once this is achieved, they wish to keep their lives as private as possible. They do not want to share their personal matters any more than Coriolanus wants to show his war wounds. It is the public and the media who determine whether and when celebrities rise and fall.

We suggest approaching this work through three key events, ending on a cliff-hanger so the story is incomplete and encourages the audience to read the rest, or watch the play in its entirety.

Part 1: Caius Martius addresses the people and war is announced.
Part 2: The battle with the Volsces.
Part 3: Caius Martius is hailed 'Caius Martius Coriolanus'.

This unit encourages and enables children to engage with and scrutinise the text, so links very closely to their literacy work. You might link this unit to work you are doing on biography where children explore the lives of famous and celebrated people, and how they have been represented. As Coriolanus is a Roman play, there are obvious links to history: if the children have studied the Greeks they will also be able to make comparisons between Coriolanus and characters from myths and legends such as Heracles or Theseus.

Key learning

Key learning for drama

By the end of this unit, the children will have:

- created a setting through independent and group improvisation;
- developed an individual character through improvisation;
- explored, spoken and acted Shakespeare's language;
- carefully considered the way certain lines should be delivered, to whom they should be directed and the possible responses;
- applied the story to a modern setting;
- worked in pairs, and then as a whole class, to develop ideas for a battle in performance.

Primary Framework for literacy objectives

- Speaking – use and explore the different ways that words are used.
- Group discussion and interaction – plan and manage a group task over time using different levels of planning.

- Drama – reflect on how working in role helps to explore complex issues; perform a scripted scene making use of dramatic conventions; use and recognise the impact of theatrical effects in drama.
- Understand and interpret texts – infer writers' perspectives from what is written and from what is implied.

Resources

Because this performance will explore the relationship between the crowd and Coriolanus, the space will need to be large enough for the crowd to form and reshape itself as the action takes place. Ideally it should include different levels (stage blocks or benches will suffice) with a central platform where Coriolanus can deliver his speeches.

Steps for teaching and learning, part 1: Caius Martius meets the people

Step 1: The airport

We suggest using a modern context to explore the themes in Coriolanus. Rather than using the whole text, picking out key lines and speeches is all that is needed. A useful place to set the action could be an airport, where fans and paparazzi are waiting for the celebrity Caius Martius to arrive. Choosing this backdrop will allow you to explore a spectrum of characters developed through improvisation.

Ask children to 'Step into the frame'. They are going to make a still image of a scene at an airport, before a celebrity arrives. Talk beforehand about the range of characters you might have, such as adoring fans who have waited for hours to see them, reporters from press and television, security guards, or young children with parents going on holiday.

Begin by asking two children to step into the central part of the picture. You can provide the first example of what the characters

137

could be – camera operators or photographers are always a good suggestion because they provide an invisible frame for the action. Then invite the class to move into the picture, one by one or in pairs. Remind them that they can join onto someone in the picture and encourage them to offer something that others could connect to, such as an outstretched hand or a hand over the mouth to suggest a secret conversation. Right from this first activity, encourage sense of audience. Wherever they choose to stand, it should provide a clear image to those who are watching.

Step 2: Bringing the picture to life

Now the still picture can come alive. Every child has a unique character that they can explore through improvisation. A good way to start this movement is to choose one child to play someone passing the picture, trailing their baggage along. As the child passes each character in the scene, they come to life one by one, reacting to one another, but the subject of their talk can only be about the awaited celebrity. Before the action begins, model how the characters might react to one another – how people who have never met before might speak to each other because of their excitement, anticipation or confusion.

Step 3: Enter Caius Martius

Caius Martius can now enter the scene. The moment before he arrives, many of the characters will be pushing as far forward as they can to be close to him, some of them will find a space way in front of the crowd as the reporters and camera operators struggle to capture the whole scene. Some may nonchalantly stand to the side. Security guards may have a very challenging job as they work together to hold the crowds back. The chatter and pushing should reach a crescendo as Caius Martius appears. He then silences the cacophony with Shakespeare's powerful words:

> MENENIUS: (A general and close friend of Caius Martius)
> Hail, noble Martius!

MARTIUS: Thanks. – What's the matter, you dissentious rogues,
That rubbing the poor itch of your opinion make yourself scabs?
(FIRST CITIZEN): We have ever your good word.
MARTIUS: He that will give good word to thee will flatter
Beneath abhorring. What would you have, you curs
That like not peace nor war? The one affrights you,
The other makes you proud. He that trusts you
Where he should find you lions finds you hares,
Where foxes, geese. You are no surer, no,
Than is the coal of fire upon the ice,
Or hailstone in the sun. Who deserves greatness
Deserves your hate, and your affections are
A sick man's appetite, who desires most that
Which would increase his evil.
Hang ye! Trust ye?
With every minute you do change a mind
And call him noble that was now your hate,
Him vile that was your garland. What's the matter,
That in these several places of the city
You cry against the noble senate, who,
Under the gods, keep you in awe, which else
Would feed on one another?
(*To Menenius*) What's their seeking?

When Caius Martius enters, he can move around the different groups
and individuals in the crowd directing lines to certain characters in
particular. Ask the children to offer suggestions for which lines can
be directed to which people. For example, one group of children with
whom we worked thought that 'like not peace nor war' should be
directed at the security guards. The 'Hang ye! Trust ye?' line was
directed at jostling reporters who moved in more aggressively to
record his words. 'The one affrights you, the other makes you proud',
was directed to an old gentleman, standing aloof, reading a
newspaper, which he rustled disapprovingly at Martius' words.

139

Step 4: A messenger brings news

The action will accelerate when the next lines are delivered: the news that 'The Volsces are in arms'. This means war.

> MARTIUS: Get you home, you fragments
> *Enter a messenger hastily*
> MESSENGER: Where's Caius Martius?
> MARTIUS: Here. What's the matter?
> MESSENGER: The news is sir, the Volsces are in arms.
> (We would suggest a cut here to ...)
> MARTIUS: They have a leader,
> Tullus Aufidius, that will put you to't.
> I sin in envying his nobility,
> And were I any thing but what I am,
> I would wish me only he.
> COMINIUS (A GENERAL): You have fought together!
> MARTIUS: He is a lion that I am proud to hunt.

You will need to take time to explore the language with the children, but the setting you have established together should help them to place it in context. So the line 'Get you home, you fragments' should get strong reactions from the crowd: disbelief, grunts of annoyance – all this helps to create a dynamic atmosphere on the stage. But the 'Volsces are in arms' line is particularly interesting. What will you and your class want the characters to do here? How will the news spread through the crowd? Will the line be repeated one by one as people hear it and pass it on to the next person? How will the media react? After all, for reporters this is history in the making and the moment recorded would make fantastic television. And when Martius has the news of war, will he still want the people and the press out of the way, or will he now want his opinions to be broadcast? You can decide with your class whether some or all of the crowd will follow him to war.

Steps for teaching and learning, part 2: The battle with the Volsces

Step 5: Creating the battle

In this part of the play, Martius will meet Aufidius in battle. In the first part, the children had to create a crowd waiting for Martius to arrive, here their characters change to soldiers at battle.

Start to develop the characters of the soldiers through the game 'The Wooden Sword of Paris'. The children work in pairs. Emphasise that there is no bodily contact, just words, actions and reactions.

Number one calls out a fighting action, for example, '*A blow to the head!*' Number one follows this call with an action, in this case he or she might make a dramatic swiping movement towards the opponent's head. Because number two has heard the call before the action, this has given them time to think about how to react and respond after the action: for example, they might duck, or lurch backwards. After their response, number two must answer the action, focusing on a different area of the body, for example, '*A dagger to the chest!*' Number one responds before making their own next move. Through this game, pairs of children build up sequences of dynamic, exciting fighting movements which are highly disciplined and safe to perform.

Step 6: Fighting together

You can now divide the whole class into two, one half being the Volsces, the other, the Romans. The two halves should be arranged like two triangles facing the centre of the room. Aufidius should be at the tip of the Volsce triangle, Martius at the tip of the Romans. You can ask the children to recall some of the phrases they used in the game to help to think of the calls and the actions. This time, Martius will call out a battle action, for example, '*A swipe to the thigh!*' He will then make the action, and all the characters behind him will copy this. Then Aufidius will react and all the characters behind will copy him. He will then call out something in response and the sequence will build.

Step 7: Developing the scene

Eventually, the children can perform the actions without words, and the spectacle can be carefully choreographed. For example, the fight may begin as two sides, each acting simultaneously, but then individual soldiers can move out of the main body and fight with a partner. Some will stand and some will fall. It is up to you how simple or complicated you want to make the battle, or how true to the text, but there must be a moment where Martius has to fight Aufidius alone. To begin with, they fight man to man, but then some Volsces come to the aid of Aufidius.

> MARTIUS: I will fight with none but thee, for I do hate thee more than a promise breaker.
> AUFIDIUS: We hate alike.
> Not Afric owns a serpent I abhor
> More than thy fame and envy. Fix thy foot.
> The stage directions say: *Martius fights till the Volsces be driven in breathless.*

The Volsces, and their leader Aufidius, are forced to retreat. Rome has taken control of Corioles. This leads to the third and final part of the performance.

Steps for teaching and learning, part 3: Martius is given the title 'Coriolanus'

Step 8: Interviewing Volumnia

Just as the play began with a large gathering, so the original crowd should be present towards the end of the play. Your actors return to the characters they played in the first scene. A class we worked with chose to open the scene with a reporter who stood in front of the crowd and interviewed Volumnia (Coriolanus' mother) and Menenius. The reporter took some of Menenius' lines from the original text.

> REPORTER: God save your good worships. Martius is coming home. He has more cause to be proud. (*To Volumnia*) Where is he wounded?
> VOLUMNIA: I'th shoulder and in the left arm. There will be large cicatrices to show the people when he shall stand for his place. He received in the repulse of Tarquin seven hurts i'th' body.
> MENENIUS: One I'th' neck and two I'th' thigh – there's nine that I know.
> VOLUMNIA: He had before this last expedition twenty five wounds upon him.
> REPORTER (TO THE CAMERA): (So) now it's twenty seven. Every gash was an enemy's grave.

The class we worked with portrayed little children pretending to battle as they heard about the wounds, the mothers and adoring female followers shook their heads with worry and concern, and consoled each other. Some of the male characters stood back with their arms folded, whilst others waved their fists in the air, saluting his victory.

Another reporter then took the Herald's line, announcing to the camera:

> HERALD: Know Rome, that all alone Martius did fight
> Within Corioles' gates, where he hath won
> With fame a name to 'Martius Caius'; these
> In honour follows 'Coriolanus'.
> Welcome to Rome renowned Coriolanus!

The newly hailed Coriolanus can exit through the crowd – it would work well if he showed distaste at their attempts to pat him on the back and wish him well. The class we worked with decided to follow this with a private exchange between Coriolanus and his mother. This suggests some of the problems that will be encountered later on in the play.

> VOLUMNIA: I have lived
> To see inherited my very wishes,
> And the buildings of my fancy. Only
> There's one thing wanting, which I doubt not but
> Our Rome will cast upon thee
> CORIOLANUS: Know, good mother
> I would rather be their servant in my way
> Than sway with them in theirs

This same group of children then concluded the play with a television report, written in their own words. Through it, they posed the question of whether Coriolanus would be able to ask the crowd to receive further honours and become consul. (This picked up on Volumnia's line – 'There's one thing wanting'.) Encouraging children to use their own words at the end of the play will allow them to include elements of the story that are still to come, but also to think about how they will leave the audience wondering about what will happen next. The aim should be to encourage their audience to leave with a desire to see or read the rest of the play.

Guidance on assessment

Any assessment of this work will be related back to the Key learning for drama, which stated that by the end of this unit the children will have:

- created a character and setting through independent and group improvisation – *are the children able to develop and refine the characters they have created through rehearsal? Do they respond to other characters and to the action?*
- explored, spoken and acted Shakespeare's language – *who seems most comfortable with this? Are they able to interpret lines in a variety of ways?*

- applied the story to a modern setting – *in discussion, do the children recognise comparisons and contrasts with their society and the story of Coriolanus?*
- worked in pairs, and then as a whole class, to develop ideas for a battle in performance – *how well do the children use space on stage? Do they show an awareness of how to create an effective visual spectacle?*

Adapting this unit

This play will challenge the most able Year 6 children, and you are unlikely to use it with younger ones. But the idea of taking two or three key scenes, exploring and presenting them as outlined here, could be used with many other plays.

Appendix 1

Drama structures and strategies used throughout the book

Guided tours

Played in pairs, one player leads their partner (whose eyes are closed) through an imaginary landscape, describing what they see as they go. We often use this in conjunction with a 'word carpet' which offers the leaders plenty of words and phrases to support their language. See, for example, Unit 4L, *Theseus and the Minotaur*.

Improvising dialogue

Usually done in pairs, the children take roles and improvise the conversation that happens between them. This can often lead to writing, perhaps putting the dialogue into a story, or writing it for a playscript. See, for example, Unit 4F, Space.

Make me a ...

A game that encourages spontaneity and creativity in groups. The teacher calls out 'Make me a ...' followed by an object or idea like a straight line, a circle, or perhaps 'Make me fear'. See, for example, Unit 6L, *Leon and the Place Between*.

Meeting in role

The children sustain their roles while they meet together and discuss what has happened in the story/drama and what they should do about it. See, for example, Unit 3F, *Dr Xargle's Book of Earthlets* and the 'alien summit'.

Soundscapes

Using their voices, sounds they can make with their bodies, everyday objects and/or musical instruments, children create mood and atmosphere with sound. See, for example, Unit 4L, *Theseus and the Minotaur*.

Still images or tableaux

A very widely used strategy in which children make pictures using themselves. These might show people doing something, or they may be more abstract as in Unit 5C, Howard Carter and Tutankhamen.

Teacher in role

The teacher takes a specific role within the drama and engages in 'live' action with the children. It is a very powerful strategy from which you can question, challenge and extend children's thinking and understanding as, for example, in Unit 4C, Change in the environment.

The Wooden Sword of Paris

A game in which children choreograph fight moves. They play it in pairs, one calling out a move – for example, 'A blow to the head!' – before making a move to go with it. The second player then speaks and moves in response. All the actions are mimed and there is no physical contact between the players. This game is used and explained more fully in Unit 6P, *Coriolanus* and also in 3C, The Romans.

147

Word carpets

Words and phrases developed through the drama are written on scraps of paper and put out on the floor to create a 'carpet'. These might be used to create a setting, or developed further into mood and atmosphere as in, for example, Unit 4L, *Theseus and the Minotaur*. They are very useful resources for later writing.

Appendix 2

Further reading to help develop drama in your school

Ackroyd, J. and Boulton, J. *Drama Lessons for Five to Eleven-year-olds.*
David Fulton 2001. Highly practical, detailed and well-structured lesson
plans, some for this age group.

Dickinson, R. and Neelands, J. *Improve Your Primary School Through Drama.*
David Fulton 2006. A detailed and uplifting account of how one inner-
city primary school placed drama at the heart of its curriculum with
remarkable results. Plenty of practical advice and examples.

Winston, J. *Drama and English at the Heart of the Primary Curriculum.* David
Fulton 2004. Detailed plans with thorough underpinning theory.
Examples are included for all the primary age groups.

Winston, J. and Tandy, M. *Beginning Drama 4–11.* David Fulton, 3rd
edition 2008. A very practical guide, aimed at those who are new to
teaching drama and designed to lead you through the process step-by-
step.

Index

Printed in Great Britain
by Amazon